THE

LONG WAY

AROUND

LEON MECHAM

a memoir

You will find what you're looking for.

to Renee, the finest woman I have ever met.

Acknowledgements

I sincerely thank my dear friends, Drs. Jim and Pam Spruiell.
Dr. Jim Spruiell was the greatest teacher I ever had.
The knowledge I gained from his guidance has touched
every area of my life, and I would not be the same man
I am today without having known the Spruiells.
Thanks also to my editor, Karen Slade Bryant,
whose genuine interest in my story and passion
for her work helped me reach the finish line!

Disclaimer

Unless a person gave me permission to
use his or her real name, the names
in my story have been changed.

Contents

Prologue

The last time I spoke to my mother, I was about fifty years old. That was more than twenty years ago. She told me she wished I were dead. My whole life, she'd blamed me for all her ails, saying my large size at birth (nine pounds, ten ounces) injured her for life. She reminded me of this as often as she could. Not surprisingly, I felt guilty. I did everything I could to please her, but she hated me until the day she died.

My parents must have come by their coldness naturally. When I was about nine and had come in from working all day in and around the barn, my grandmother told me, "You smell like a skunk." She never had a kind word for me, never showed me any affection. But that was life in our house with my parents, grandparents, and siblings: no hugs, no kisses, no love. I never saw my father and mother hug or show any affection toward one another.

Grandpa and Grandma, my father's parents, moved onto the farm with us when I was about nine. This had to have been a hard move for them, as Mom and Dad treated them with the same disdain and disrespect they showed me. Nevertheless, Grandpa and Grandma moved their Airstream travel trailer onto the farm, which was owned by my father's boss. Dad's boss gave us a steer to raise each year for our beef, and we raised chickens and turkeys, even a hog for our pork. We had a large garden, and we raised and canned vegetables and fruits. Grandpa and I would go to the woods and hunt for morel mushrooms, the greatest mushroom God ever created. We'd find wild greens like poke greens, which were very tasty. We had no rent to pay and very little groceries to buy. But Dad got paid so little as a farm manager, we still lived in poverty.

During the summers, I worked full time building fences, hauling hay, feeding calves, feeding the stud bulls, and working the family garden. Dad's boss gave me a registered Holstein heifer for payment. My dad sold it without a word of thanks or acknowledgement to me. The next summer, the same thing happened. I worked, got paid with a heifer, and Dad sold the heifer, which came from the stock we had on the farm.

Dad's boss named his operation Paganock Farms. The farm was home to Wonder Gingerbread Betty, the cow that set a world record for producing milk. Paganok was also home to the cow that held the world record in butterfat production. The cows, bulls, and heifers on Paganok Farms were some of the most expensive dairy cows on the planet. My father, demonstrating what I saw as extremely shortsighted and poor judgment, sold these two potentially record-setting heifers for a pittance and lost a great opportunity to develop his own herd. In the meantime, Mom and Dad made my grandparents give them their social security checks to use for food, cigarettes, and whatever else, but my parents somehow never had anything to show for that money, either. We were so poor, we could expect cheap socks and cheap underwear at Christmas and on our birthdays.

Some of the things I saw my mother do left me wondering about her mental capacity. One incident has stayed with me my whole life. When I was about five, we bought a new gas oven. Mother, attempting to light the oven, had turned on the gas, and with the gas turned on, she stuck her head inside the oven and lit a match. I was standing about twenty feet away when the explosion blew my mother out of the oven and set her hair on fire. I can see it as vividly today in my memory as I saw it then.

While a genius-level IQ is not imperative to living a decent life, both my parents made what was in my opinion, some epic bad decisions, the worst I have ever seen anybody make.

If these two weren't challenged enough, when I was about nine and my older sister was twelve, my sister was diagnosed with cancer of the ovaries. At that time, in 1959, the American Medical Association knew almost nothing about cancer. In fact, my sister's first diagnosis was pregnancy. The first wave of doctors wasn't too sharp, but what should we have expected, being raised in Hillbilly country? I laugh when I tell people that when I graduated from a university, I elevated my social status from Hillbilly to Redneck! I'm proud to be a Redneck!

My sister's prognosis was that she might have a few months to live. She lived for twenty-plus years after that. She was, and still is, my hero. She never whined or complained, even after a dozen or more surgeries.

Throughout all this, we attended the Mormon church regularly and frequently. Mormons held lots of meetings: Sunday School on Sunday morning, Sacrament meeting on Sunday evening, and some type of a meeting/worship on Wednesday evening. Before Sunday School there was a men-only meeting for members of the Melchizedek Priesthood, which the church said acted as the power and authority of God. Priesthood is conferred upon male members the church deems worthy. The priesthood had offices of Elder, the Seventies, and the High Priest. My father was an Elder in the

Melchizedek Priesthood, and with that title came responsibilities. He was charged with home teaching, the laying on of hands for the sick, and supporting the church and activities. Then there was the Relief Society, a women's organization. I don't remember a lot about the Relief Society, but I do recall that once, when I accidentally stumbled into their area, I saw an abundance of cookies, pies, and cakes. The women also had responsibilities such as visiting the sick and needy. With my first wife attending these meetings, I picked up on a lot of gossip. Everybody knew who was sick, whose children were misbehaving, who had become inactive, and countless other details of other people's lives.

We prayed a lot. We had a family prayer before we drove anywhere. At the beginning of every meeting, we had prayer, and at the end of the meeting we prayed again. We had a special prayer for the sick. There were the special prayers we said when anointing the sick with olive oil. The oil was considered sacred, and a couple of members of the Melchizedek Priesthood were required to say a prayer for it, also. After five to ten prayers a day, I saw nothing ever change for the better.

When we prayed, we were always asking God to do something. I felt that God did not give a crap about us. We used the same language that other Mormons used in their meetings. The intro, content, and salutation used distinctively Mormon words. In those days we performed our saying of pledge of allegiance to the American flag and prayed before class at school. My prayers were Mormon based and were different from the prayers the other kids said. It singled me out as different from the rest of the class.

At school and at home, we said prayers over our food. The first Sunday of the month was a special day, as it was designated for fasting. This was a day also reserved to spend in prayer and reading the scriptures. Typically, we ate Saturday night and did not eat again until Monday morning.

The pantry and refrigerator were often bare, as we didn't have money to buy groceries. We did, however, always have gas money to drive all those miles to all those damn meetings! We lived in the country, which meant we had to drive anywhere from ten miles to seventy-five miles one way, depending on how far out we lived at any given time.

Mom and Dad always had good Sunday "go-to-meetin'" clothes. I usually wore holy clothes, as my socks and underwear often had holes in them. Dad always had a nice-looking suit, a white shirt, and nice leather lace-up shoes. I was growing fast, and my pants' legs usually fell above my ankles, while my sleeves fell somewhere between my wrists and my elbows. By the time I was twelve, I was as tall as my father.

I was always the tallest kid in my class at the country schools. When I was in the fifth grade, my sisters and I attended Bates school. It was a one-room schoolhouse where first graders sat in the first row; eighth graders were in the eighth row, and so on. To get to the schoolhouse, my sisters and I would walk out the back door of our old two-story farmhouse, walk by the chicken house and hog pens, across the back pasture, then walk a mile or two down a dirt road. The school had two, two-hole wooden outhouses, one for the boys and one for the girls. We had the same outhouse design at home.

When I was in sixth grade, we moved, and we attended Palmyra schools. Classes numbered twenty or so in each grade. This was a city school, although we still lived quite a few miles from town. I attended this school during my sixth and seventh grades. We rode the bus. I was just as tall and skinny as ever. My classmates for the next few years tried to give me nicknames, like Lurch, or honest Abe.

When I entered my teenage years, I was so skinny that you could count my ribs from fifty feet away.

My father was very unstable. From the time I entered the first grade at five years old until I graduated from high school at seventeen years old, I had attended twelve schools. The dark cloud of depression set in hard during my senior year. I thought about running away from home numerous times, but had no direction, so I stayed home.

The high school I attended was in a small town and was B-rated. My junior class had thirty-five students. I was voted most popular. I was class treasurer. I wrote an article for the class newspaper. I played the clarinet in the school band. I was the escort to the homecoming queen, was the top rebounder on the basketball team and top scorer. Our football team was so bad that we had our homecoming celebration during basketball season.

We lived in this place for two and a half years. I played all the sports. The first summer, I played baseball. I wasn't particularly good, as I had never played a team sport of any kind. The coach put me in center field on defense. I was good at catching the ball but failed at hitting it. This coach, for some reason, took a disliking to me. I was never allowed to bat during batting practice. One game, he put me in center field. The batter hit the ball almost straight up, and when I tried to catch it, I lost sight of it in the sun. Coach immediately jerked me out of the game and gave me a go-to-hell look. I was replaced by another player, of course. When the next batter hit, the same thing happened. The batter hit the ball into the sun; the fielder missed it. But the coach left that player in. I looked at the coach and gave him my look. I quit the team and went to work the rest of the summer hauling hay with some Cherokee Indians. My sister was dating one of the guys, and I liked to hang with my older sister when I could.

Fall came, and most of the boys I had met were friendly and accepting. They talked me into playing football, as a twelve-man football team in a B-rated school needs everybody physically able to participate. I was slow when it came to sprints and short distances but could easily run four miles with my long, skinny legs and torso. So, Coach decided to have me take the football as a running back and run around the left end. The coach himself tackled me by hitting me in my right knee, effectively shattering my kneecap, dislocating my knee joint, and tearing some interior ligaments. I was about fourteen. I was furious with him for years after that. My parents pretty much left me alone to take care of myself other than to take me to the doctor when needed. They couldn't have cared less that a grown man had disabled their son for life.

Finally, many, many years later, I was able to negotiate a deal with an orthopedic surgeon and had arthroscopic surgery on both knees. The doctor removed bone fragments that had lodged under and around my right kneecap. My interior ligament was stretched so severely that the doctor had to make an adjustment to shorten it and repair torn tissue.

I harbored anger at my old coach until I realized that all that pain and suffering kept me out of Vietnam. Believe it or not, I thanked him for that, as the war got really ugly during the time I would have been drafted. That coach might have saved my life; so I quit being angry at him.

In high school, I was doing well in basketball. My coach was talking with me about my talent and future, and he was talking with recruits at the University of Arkansas. By my junior year, I was getting really good and led our little basketball team to district finals.

Then, another move changed everything. We were moving for the twelfth time since I'd started first grade. I had friends, girlfriends, and a promising future. Facing reality, though, I knew my knees were in no shape to play college ball. I had had a couple of invitations to attend a college practice, but I knew my knees would not hold up for the long haul.

We moved to Joplin, Missouri. My senior class had approximately 500 students. I tried to get into basketball there, but I was no longer the tallest guy around. There were a few others as tall as I was, and there was one who was a lot taller. Also, these city boys had been playing together since they were in middle school. If I had tried really hard and improved, I might have been able to play as the twelfth man on the team. The basketball team was so good, in fact, we won the Missouri State Championship in 5-A basketball.

I was severely depressed. I hated school and did as little as possible in hopes I would just graduate. I wanted to go back to Arkansas, so I packed my clothes, got into my car, and left Missouri for Arkansas. Mom or Dad called the local authorities and the state police. Grandpa had seen me carrying my stuff to the car and told my mom. I was caught in Arkansas and informed by my mother that she was on the way to get me and that if I tried to run again, they would place me in a home for juvenile delinquents. I had already been cutting classes, and now I missed more classes. The principal assigned thirty-two detention halls for me to serve for poor behavior. That was an hour a day after classes! I went to a few then quit going. I should have failed because of my poor grades, but I guess the principal and teachers wanted to be rid of me, so they allowed me to graduate.

I was depressed, confused, and still growing physically. I took on a job that paid minimum wage. Then that summer a member of our local ward informed me that he and his family were moving to Fort Lauderdale, Florida. He asked me if I was interested in driving his

Mustang to Florida. He needed me and a friend to transport his wife and daughter. He promised me and my friend a job in return. Let's see, I thought, "Go to Florida, get away from my parents… hell, yes!"

The man who made the offer went ahead of us to get his business finalized, and we were to drive his car, his wife, and his infant daughter to meet him in Fort Lauderdale two weeks later. But when we got there, there was no job! This good Mormon man had lied to us and played us kids for suckers.

My friend's mother lived in Miami, so he called her. She drove to Fort Lauderdale, picked us up, and took us back home with her. In Miami, I worked at a grocery store as a bagger for a while, then heard about a job at a lumber yard. I went to work there and unloaded semi-trucks when they came to resupply. I also waited on customers in the lumber area. After I'd been there a few weeks, my friend borrowed a few dollars from me, and when my mother called to tell me that my dad had had a heart attack and was in the hospital, I tried to collect from my friend the money he owed me. He refused to pay, so I gave him two black eyes and a fat lip.

I got a ride to the bus station, and after almost two days riding and sleeping on the Greyhound bus, I made it back to Joplin. Dad had been driving a semi-rig, hauling produce across the country. He had crossed over into Tijuana and had bought some illegal drugs. This good scripture-quoting, abusing man now smuggled illegal drugs into California. He proceeded to drive his truck back to Joplin while he consumed amphetamines. His heart attack was caused by an overdose of illegal drugs. What a fine Mormon, I thought. My parents' hopes of going to heaven, where they'd heard the streets were paved with gold, and their dream of being among the chosen few to have the right to sit at the right hand of God seemed to me to be in stark contrast to the way they lived their lives.

I would have my trusting, naïve eyes opened even more as the years passed and as I learned about life by living it. I was an optimistic, hard-working young man eager to make my own way, but my disillusionment with family, religion, and people I wholeheartedly trusted sent me reeling, landing me in a psychological abyss I saw no way out of. The path that ultimately brought me success and happiness had its deep pits and valleys — I suffered my own addictions and faced my own demons. Mine is a story of the resilience of the human spirit, of the power we all have within ourselves to persevere and overcome.

My younger sister and I with one of
the heifers I earned as payment.

My grandparents. Grandfather Hank was more
of a mentor to me than my father was.

CHAPTER 1

Baker and Taylor Oil Field, Spearman, Texas

I'd just driven to Spearman, Texas, from Joplin, Missouri, and had spent all day — more than eight hours and four hundred and twenty-four miles — on the road. My 1962 Chevy Impala Super Sport held all my possessions, which were sparse, even for an eighteen-year-old who'd grown up in poverty, but my 305 Honda Scrambler was stuffed into the trunk, and I was a kid with a purpose: I was about to have my first real job. Oh, I'd worked before — at sixteen, I'd helped run a burger joint back home, but I'd done nothing that could have prepared me for the adventure that lay ahead.

I found the door to the workshop and opened it. I had spoken with a representative from Baker and Taylor Oil Co. a couple of days before and had been told I'd have a job as soon as I could get there. A ray of light drew my eye to the night foreman, who was busy at his worktable. I shyly introduced myself and explained that I'd been hired. The foreman gave me directions to a nearby hotel, where he said I'd be staying for the night on the company's dime. I was to report back to the main office in the morning.

As I headed to the address the foreman had given me, I thought of the circumstances that had brought me here. My father was in the hospital recovering from a heart attack. My mother had sent me, the wet-behind-the-ears second eldest of four children, to the oil fields to earn money to support the family.

I spotted a telephone booth and stopped. It was dark, but a streetlamp shed enough light for me to see the coin slot on the pay phone, and I slid a dime in, dialed zero, and waited for the operator.

"I want to place a collect, person-to-person call to Leon," I said, and gave the operator the number, just as Mother had told me to do.

The operator dialed the number, and when my mother answered, the operator said, "Hello. I have a collect call for Leon."

"Leon isn't here," my mother responded.

"There is no one there by the name of Leon," the operator told me. "Is there anyone else you wish to speak to?"

"No, thank you," I answered. Without speaking to anyone and without paying for a long-distance call, I'd let my family know that I'd safely arrived in Texas. I also knew that saving even the cost of a phone call was important. My family was poor. Neither parent had gone to school past the sixth grade. My father could drive a truck, but neither he nor my mother had any specific training or marketable skills.

My parents had their sights set on going to heaven, and they believed the Mormons could get them there. They also believed that poor people stood a better chance of entering the Pearly Gates, so they had chosen a lifestyle of poverty.

I found the weathered hotel and was reminded of the old farmhouses I'd grown up in. The moon was coming out and provided enough light for me to see that the wood siding was cupping and showing signs of rot. The paint and siding were coming off. Open windows exposed tattered curtains. Run-down cars and old pickups filled the small parking lot and lined the curb out front. I parked and went inside. I had never stayed in, or even been inside of, a hotel. Once when we'd taken a trip, I'd slept in the car with my parents and sisters, but that was as close to "lodging" outside of home that I'd ever experienced.

I entered a common area furnished with tables and chairs and could see that I'd have to navigate through some rough-looking men — some standing around the check-in counter, a few sitting in the chairs and on the couch — to get to the counter. The men looked very comfortable, as if this were their place, and I, a skinny, squeaky-clean kid, had entered their home uninvited. I felt like a high-school nerd walking into a bikers' rally. Most of the men were unshaven, dirty, and greasy. It was the nastiest, dirtiest, and roughest looking group I had ever encountered. They were loud, many of them drunk, shoving each other around, laughing and talking boisterously.

These men, as I would come to learn, were known in the area as oil field trash. The room fell quiet, and all eyes were upon me. I felt extremely self-conscious, like my skin was on fire, and then suddenly, my mind was flooded with memories. I remembered my father coming in from the grain fields, filthy, smelly, and angry — just like these men — and I remembered the beatings he'd give me. The lobby carried the stench of the oil rig (a smell I would soon come to know very well) and reeked of body odor, cigarette smoke, and alcohol. I crinkled my nose, trying to keep the smell from getting into my nostrils as I made my way to the counter.

"Yeah? What do you want here, boy?" the hotel clerk addressed me.

"I just came from the Baker and Taylor office, and the foreman told me to come here. I need a room." I could feel my legs begin to shake, and my heart was pounding.

14

"Sure thing."

The clerk checked his ledger and had me sign in.

"The foreman said that Baker and Taylor would pay the bill," I offered.

"Yep," was the terse reply.

The clerk handed me the key to 205 and told me how to get upstairs where, because of space limitations, I would be sleeping in the same room with other men. As I turned from the counter to make my way across the lobby to the stairs, the dirtiest of the oil field workers stepped in front of me. The man's dark, greasy hair was falling into his eyes; his T-shirt was stained brown and black, and I wouldn't have been surprised if his filthy pants had stood up and walked on their own. On the man's unshaven face was a wicked grin that revealed missing teeth. His stench made me want to back away, but I stood my ground.

"And just what the hell do you think you're doing here?" he growled. Like one of my grandfather's favorite expressions, I didn't know whether to shit or go blind. I was consumed by fear, my legs unsteady and quivering, my heart pounding. I was a stranger among strangers. I had lived the strict life of a good Mormon boy and had never been exposed to men like these. But I reminded myself that I was there to do a job, to uphold my responsibility to my family. I paused a second to gather myself, then boldly spoke directly into the man's face, telling him about my father and that I'd come to work for my family. I might have lacked experience, but I knew I could show no weakness. I prayed that my shaking legs would not give me away.

The man glared at me as he spoke: "Listen, boy, we were just talking about the main cable that broke on Rig One yesterday. Ten tons of blocks and tackle fell and landed on a floor hand. He had blood coming out of his mouth that bubbled as he moaned from the pain. He lived until they were able to move the blocks off him two and a half hours later; then he died."

He shoved his face closer to mine to make his point. "The best thing for you to do is to get your skinny ass in your car and get the hell back home."

I felt that my bowels might turn loose any second. I had been taught to put my family first and foremost. I believed in what I was doing, and that gave me strength. I found the courage to inform the man in no uncertain terms that I would be staying.

Exhausted and nearly overwhelmed by fear, I made my way up to the communal bedroom. I found an empty bed with clean but threadbare sheets and settled in for the night. Convinced I'd be stabbed or shot in my sleep, I opened my eyes every time I heard a creak or squeak. I didn't sleep a wink.

I got up the next morning, showered, shaved, and returned to the office of Baker and Taylor.

The secretary was expecting me. "I have some forms for you," she said. "Please complete them and return them to me. You may sit over there." She handed me a clipboard and a pen and pointed to a chair near the front window.

"Here's Red's phone number and address," she said. "He's the driller in charge of the rig you are assigned to work on. You'll need to call him for further instructions. Do you have a place to stay?"

"No, ma'am."

"Here's the address of a place downtown on the square. The owner rents apartments on the second floor, over the businesses downstairs."

I thanked her for the information.

I found the address and followed a narrow stairwell to the second level, set between a hardware store and an insurance office.

I found the landlady, introduced myself, and told her I needed an apartment. She motioned for me to follow her. We reached an apartment, and the landlady opened the door. "The rent is $50 a month," she said. "This is the only room available."

The apartment had two rooms — a kitchen/eating area and a bedroom. There was a shared bathroom down the hall for all tenants on the second floor. The apartment was rundown and sparsely furnished, but it was clean.

"What comes with the room?" I asked. "I don't see any sheets or pillows."

"You are furnished pots, pans, and eating ware. I'll see if I can find some sheets and pillows for you," the landlady offered grudgingly.

"Thank you," I said.

I went downstairs, found a telephone booth, and dialed the number I'd been given for Red.

"Hello?"

"Hello, is this Red?" I asked.

"Yes, what can I do for you?"

"My name is Leon, and I was told to call you. I was told that I would be on your crew."

"That's great," the man said. "Where can I pick you up?"

I gave Red my new address.

"Evening tower shift starts at 4 p.m. I'll be there to pick you up around 2:30. Be sure to pack some food."

"Thank you, sir. I'll be ready."

I then dialed the number to my home, hoping to speak to my mother.

"Hello, Mom?"

"Please deposit $1.50," the operator instructed.

I slipped six quarters into the slot and spoke as quickly as I could. I had paid for only three minutes.

"Mom, I made it and checked in with the company. I have the job! I called my supervisor, the driller, and he's going to pick me up and take me to the rig later. I also have a room that costs me $50 a month. I'll be working seven nights a week, eight hours a night, from 4 p.m. until midnight. They call this shift the evening tower shift. They asked me if I was willing to work extra shifts, as they're so shorthanded. I told them I was. I'm earning $3.50 an hour, and I can work a couple of extra shifts a week. I get time and a half for anything over forty hours and double time for any time over sixty hours. I'll send as much home as I can. How is Dad?"

"The doctor says your father is doing as well as could be expected and should be out of the hospital soon," Mother replied. "Stay out of trouble, son."

I found the post office and rented a box to receive mail, then I stocked up on a few items at the grocery store. I carried only 175 pounds on my six-feet, four-inch frame, and like most 18-year-old boys, I could put away a lot of calories. I would be so hungry at times I would cook an entire pound of bacon, scramble a dozen eggs, and eat it all with some toast and milk. My father was often amazed by how much food I could consume. He would say that my legs must be hollow and that was where all the food ended up.

When I returned to my room, the landlady was in the hallway with a bundle in her hands.

"I found a set of sheets and a couple of towels you can use," she said.

"Thank you, Ms. Winters. I really appreciate this."

"I even found a couple of dish towels. Do you need anything else?"

"No. I think I'm good for now. I picked up a few things at the store."

"I heard this will be your first day."

"Yes, ma'am."

"You'll be fine. Just be careful, and always watch what you are doing. I've heard some ugly stories involving accidents."

"Yes, ma'am. I will take care. Thank you."

I carried the clean towels and sheets into my room.

A dark spot on the old, worn beige carpet made me think that someone must have spilled a glass of wine there. I had heard that wine stains everything. The kitchen held a tiny gas range with the smallest oven I had ever seen. The refrigerator was old and small; the bedroom was barely big enough to hold the single twin bed against the wall. The bathroom down the hall had a pedestal sink, commode, and small shower, with the shower head positioned so that I would have to lean over and bend my knees to wash my hair. But I didn't need anything fancy — just somewhere to fix a meal or two, take shower, and lay my head. My feet were on their own, though, as they hung off the end of the bed.

Raised as a farm hand, I'd spent most of my adolescence in the hay barn, milk barn, on a tractor, or in the field hauling hay. I was eight years old when I first drove a tractor. I had always relied on my mom to shop for groceries and prepare meals. Occasionally, I would fix my own breakfast or make a sandwich, but now, I had to do all the grocery shopping, cooking, and cleaning myself. Growing up so poor, I couldn't always count on getting an evening meal, and I had gone to bed hungry many a night. With my parents' belief that money was evil, they never pursued ways to improve their circumstances. But I thought that money was great; it bought clothes that fit, cars that ran, and other nice things.

As 2:30 that afternoon approached, I headed to the sidewalk to wait for Red, who drove up in a light green, four-door 1962 Chevrolet Impala. Three other rig hands were in the car. Getting out of the car, Red introduced himself and then introduced me to the other crew members: Earl, Bear, and Willie. I guessed Red to be in his mid-forties and about five feet, ten inches tall. He had red hair, blue eyes, and ruddy, red, weathered skin. I learned that he was married, had two children, and lived in a mobile home.

It was customary for the driller to pick up the crew and drive to the rig, which could be an hour or more away. No one wanted to drive his own car, so everybody carpooled. Following his normal routine, Red stopped at the liquor store so the crew could stock up for the long night. Red bought mostly beer along with some whiskey and vodka and placed it with bags of ice into a cooler into the trunk of his car. After about an hour or so, we arrived at the rig. I stood in awe. The tower was a steel frame with cables and pulleys. It stood over 125 feet high at the crown. Red took me to the lower doghouse, which was where the crew kept personal items. It served as a kind of locker room. It was a portable steel building similar to a forty-foot storage container, but this one had benches and lockers. When the weather was really bad, this was one of the few places where we could go in and warm up, thanks to a small propane heater inside.

"Leon, come up here with me," Red said as he led me up the steps to the drilling floor and the upper doghouse where the driller's station and driller's doghouse were located. It had accommodations for the driller to do his paperwork and lie down if he needed to. This room was on the same level as the drilling floor, about ten feet above ground level. The drilling floor was where most of the blood, sweat, and tears happened.

Red took me through my duties. "This is where we keep the bags for soil samples. Come with me, and I'll show you how I want you to do this." Red picked up a bag and a pen.

"First, take a pen and fill out the date and time of each sample bag," he said. The bags looked like tobacco pouches my grandfather rolled his cigarettes in. He led me back downstairs to the ground floor and around the crew's doghouse to an area under the drilling platform at the blowout preventer, where some dirt had been removed and space was made for a small pit.

Red continued his instructions. "Each hour, on the hour, you are to reach down here in this pit and get a soil sample like this and put it into the bag. You are to do this every hour, so each shift you are to collect eight soil samples. This will tell the geologists what kind of soil or rock we are drilling in." My father had trained me to do as I was told, and this sure seemed like a simple task.

Red then reviewed other tasks I would be responsible for.

I was ready to be a part of the crew and do my part. After a couple of hours, the hands gathered by the crew's doghouse, and Bear put his arm on my left shoulder. "Leon," he said, "we need to initiate you so you can be an official 'Worm.' We're going to take your pants off and dope your balls with rig grease." New crew members were labeled worms because they were considered to be lower in life than the worms that lived underground.

I wasn't going to let anyone bully me again. I had had enough bullying from my own father. I hadn't been able to fight back when I was small, but I was grown now, and I wouldn't let anyone bully me without a fight.

"Well," I drawled, "I'm not sure how many of you it will take to do that, but know this: you might better bring all the help you can get." Everyone laughed, but the crew wasn't certain about me, and as it turned out, I was never initiated.

After we'd been on the job about six hours, the crew broke into the cooler, and everybody except Willie helped himself to a beer. Willie opted for a shot of whiskey. Bear offered me a beer. I had tasted beer before — a light, Kansas 3.5% brew, but that was the limit of my experience with alcohol. This would be my first 5% beer, so I paced myself, and by the time I got back to my place, I was doing well, but I was tired and felt a buzz from the few beers I'd had.

It didn't take long for me to develop a camaraderie with the guys. The guys might have looked motley: Bear was about six feet tall and had a very stocky frame; Earl was about six-foot-one, and also had heavy bones and a stocky build; Willie was about five feet, nine inches, and had a medium build, but all were good people. I especially liked and appreciated Red.

I was fascinated by the work, though I knew it was dangerous. Each step had to be precisely performed. My fellow crew members had made me feel welcome and part of the team.

Everything ran smoothly on our rig, which was drilling around 5,000 feet deep. Most people, and even I, thought we were drilling for oil, but in fact, we were drilling for natural gas. Infrequently, the drill bit would get dull. It would show up as a flat line on the graph that provided constant feedback; this graph was in the driller's doghouse. When the graph indicated the bit was dull, we would call the tool pusher. The tool pusher supervised the drillers and was in charge of a number of rigs. When the drill bit got dull, it and, of course, all the drill pipe attached above it had to come out of the hole, no matter how deep we were. Each joint of pipe was thirty feet long. The crew would take three joints out at once, so each length was taken out and vertically stacked in ninety-foot lengths. This required a crew of at least three, but we managed better with four, one man ninety feet above and three below. Our five-man crew had no problem with this task.

One day, not long after I'd started, Red told us: "Earl's not going to make it tonight, and Willie is driving his own car and will be a little late. In the meantime, we need to get this bit out of the hole, so let's get started."

The wind was blowing around twenty mph, and it was cold and raining, freezing the water on the drilling floor and creating a solid sheet of ice. Willie showed up an hour late. As he stepped onto the drilling floor, he was weaving and stumbling more so than the slippery ice would have caused. It was clear he had been drinking.

Red pulled the pipe up as Bear grabbed the cow's cock near the top of the pipe from the stabbing floor ninety feet above and unlocked it, then moved the top of the pipe over to the side of the rig and tied it off. The cow's cock was a hinged, solid steel clamp that the derrick hand used to lock onto the pipe to pull it up and lower it down. The two sets of tongs, located at the corners of the drilling floor, were large, heavy, giant pipe wrenches, and weighed some 350 pounds each. Each of the tongs was suspended from a cable so it could be swung from side to side. Willie stumbled and slid onto the drilling floor, grabbing a side rail near one of the tongs. He was making me nervous. After he slipped and fell again, I told him to get off the floor.

"I'm fine. I can do my job," he insisted.

"You're too drunk to be here, and you're going to get one or both of us hurt," I countered and turned to Red. "If you get Willie off the floor, I can run the slips and the tongs by myself." I grabbed the slips and placed the three-jointed tool into the turntable to lock the pipe in.

Red yelled to Willie: "Get the hell down to the bottom dog-house. You can't even keep yourself upright. You're going to get someone killed."

Willie left, and Red helped me a little here and there; we were doing a three-man job. Each time we broke a joint of pipe, drilling mud oozed out onto the ice, making it slicker than snot.

This job was dangerous enough on a dry floor, but with ice and mud on the floor and with alcohol numbing a worker's mind, lots of bad things could happen. These tools and tasks required quick responses, strength, balance, coordination, and agility. A crew member needed to have his full faculties about him. Over the course of an eight-hour shift, the work demanded physical endurance.

Midnight came, and although a lot of pipe had been pulled out of the hole, the morning tower crew would have to finish the job to get a new bit attached to the end of the pipe. I was exhausted after eight hours of pulling pipe, running the tongs, and setting the slips mostly by myself. I had also had to run the chain after we broke the joint loose with the tongs. The chain was used to unscrew the joint; this took coordination, speed, and strength. Many a floor hand had lost fingers, hands, or arms in throwing the chain. Although I was a willing worker, my title was still *Worm*. Every night, eight times on my shift and eight more times when I pulled a double shift, I filled out a tag on a pouch and placed into the pouch a soil sample from the circulation pit by the blowout preventer. I quickly got into the groove of all my duties.

One morning, I awoke with a headache and an unsettled stomach. I waited a little while, hoping I would feel better after I'd had a light breakfast; when that didn't help, I called Red.

"Hello, Red?"

"Good morning, Leon. What's up with you today?"

Weakly, I said "Red, I am really feeling bad, and I'm not sure I can make it to work tonight."

"I understand, and if you feel too bad to work, that's okay," Red said. "I just want you to think about this: If you stay home, you will have headaches, stomach aches, and maybe some other pain. If you come to work, you will have headaches, stomach aches, and maybe some other pain also. The difference is, if you come to work, you get paid!"

I pondered this for a moment and replied, "I'll be ready at 2:30." I was focused on taking care of my family. I needed to send money back home.

After a few weeks, I was part of the "oil field trash" family, and I loved it. The guys were jovial. They liked to drink and have a good time. My lifestyle was the polar opposite of the lifestyle I had experienced growing up. I no longer attended the Mormon church that I had been forced to attend and had been baptized into. I now freely drank caffeine-based drinks and alcohol. As a Mormon boy, I had participated in many ceremonies and rituals, and now I was questioning the lessons I had been taught. I was feeling as though I'd been brainwashed to be, act, and live like a Mormon. I had found no room for individualism in the Mormon church.

Though drinking was not a requirement to work in the oil field, it was what most everybody did — that is, when they weren't working or fighting. I had been working hard and needed as much sleep as I could get. The good thing was that I was no longer having bloody, violent nightmares, which had tortured me for years at home. I wasn't sure whether their disappearance was because of my being so tired or whether it was from my getting away from the Mormons and my family, but I was relieved that they had subsided.

We were moving to a new drilling site, so to prepare, we reported for work one morning at 8 o'clock. The hole had been drilled; the pipe had been taken out, stacked, and other parts of the rig were being taken down. A casing crew from Halliburton had begun setting the permanent casing. All members from the drilling crews had joined forces to work to rig down and rig up.

"Well, boys," said Red, "the other crews and I will finish rigging down here and finish loading up. I want you four to drive over to the new site. Bear, you're in charge. Be sure you have shovels as you will need to 'spud-in.'" To spud-in meant to displace a sufficient amount of dirt to make a two-foot-deep-by-five-feet-in-diameter pit to allow for the setting of the blowout preventer.

Willie, Bear, Earl, and I drove to the new site in Bear's black Ford Galaxy 500 and set to digging. We hadn't been working long before I noticed that Earl was not digging; he was just leaning on his shovel, watching us work.

As I dug, I kept an eye on Earl, and every time I glanced his way, I saw him just leaning on his shovel.

"Hey, asshole, you're getting paid to do some digging, too, so get with the program. I'm not digging your portion," I said to him.

"Kiss my ass. You're not my boss." Earl retorted. This was his way of bullying others, by having others do his work while he coasted. He was a fairly big man, and strong, and pretty much dared anyone to tell him what to do. He was just flat-out lazy.

I was fed up with Earl's slacking off. I stormed over to him, and we started shoving one another.

"Get to work!" I yelled as I shoved Earl.

"Up yours. You can't tell me what to do," Earl responded, shoving me back.

"I'm not doing your job so you can stand around and get paid for it. Unless, of course, you want to pay me." I remembered my grandfather's lesson about working. He taught me to always do my best. It really irritated me that Earl would have such little integrity to take payment for his labor when he was shirking his responsibility.

"I ain't giving you a dime," challenged Earl.

Earl was older and had a much stockier build, and the ground was very uneven. Earl pushed me, causing me to fall backward over a large clump of dirt. He was moving menacingly toward me when Willie and Bear stepped in. "Break it up now," they urged. "We need to get out of here; there is a snowstorm coming." We realized what was coming our way as the wind picked up, and light snow started coming in sideways.

Bear told us to gather all the shovels and picks and put them into the tool house while he got the car started and came around for us. By the time the tools were put up, it was snowing hard. We piled into Bear's black Ford Galaxy, and we headed for the dirt road. By the time we reached the dirt road about 500 yards away, the snow was drifting up to twelve inches in spots. When we reached the paved highway about three miles away, there were snowplows out working, and we headed back to town. This meant an evening off. I got home, washed dishes, and cleaned up a little. I got my dirty clothes together, went to the coin laundry, and washed clothes. Around 7 p.m., I decided to go out for a hamburger. It had quit snowing as I pulled into the local hamburger place. I'd met a cute little redheaded girl about my age not long after I'd arrived in Spearman, and she worked at the restaurant.

"Hey, how are you doing this evening?" I asked her.

"I'm good. How are you?"

"I got off work early tonight because of the weather. Would you like to go for a drive?" I offered.

"That sounds like fun. Why, yes, I guess that would be okay. I get off at 8," she agreed.

I picked her up at 8 p.m. We drove around a little and talked. I was enjoying her company. Just looking at her made me smile. Everything was going great until she mentioned that her dad was the sheriff. This spooked me so badly that I immediately drove back to town and let her out. My father had always had bad things to say about highway patrolmen and policemen. I visualized getting shot or arrested by an angry father because I'd put my arm around his daughter's shoulders. I was horrified to think that her father might take a disliking to me, so I bailed.

So much for my social life. A few days later as I was getting into Red's car, Red asked if I'd like to work another double shift, as the morning tower crew was shorthanded.

I told him I would, and he let me know that a temporary driller from Alaska would be running the rig. "He should be okay," Red said.

Again, as luck would have it, the crew had been coming out of the hole to replace a dull bit with a sharp one. The bit was at the bottom, of course, about 2,000 feet down. This meant that I would have no breaks or time-outs on my regular shift or on my double shift, because coming out of or going into the hole meant assholes and elbows from all the crew.

I had to remind the new driller to slow down the cathead, that I was having a hard time keeping up. This was definitely one of the most dangerous parts of the job — throwing the chain when breaking the joint and when making up the pipe joint. I had to be careful. I didn't want to lose any fingers.

"I was enjoying watching you work; you're really good," the driller told me.

The crew grabbed another bite on another section of pipe and pulled it up into position, and I helped set the slips. We used tongs to break the joint; then I prepared the chain.

"Hey, driller," I spoke a little louder. "I asked you to slow down that cathead." The driller was coming down hard and fast on the lever that ran the cathead. The harder the driller pulled on the lever, the faster the drum turned to take up the slack in the chain. I was getting upset. I had asked the driller to slow down, and he had ignored me. This was a major safety issue.

I stopped working. "Hey, asshole, I said slow down the god-damned cathead," I told the driller as I left the turntable area and began walking toward him. He was about fifteen feet away. Zeke, a worker from another rig, had pulled a double and was working as a derrick hand, which meant working from the stabbing board approximately ninety feet above the drill floor. He heard the commotion and saw me moving toward the driller. He knew me and knew that I didn't take any flak from anyone. With the hope of preventing a fight, Zeke quickly unhooked his safety harness, jumped onto the ninety-foot section of pipe that he had not yet racked, slid down the pipe, and just barely got between the driller and me.

"Leon, you work the stabbing board and rack the pipe, and I'll take care of the floor."

I looked around and decided to get upstairs and rack the pipe from the stabbing floor. I had been working hard that night, and I was tired and cranky, but I had avoided a major physical confrontation. I was not only new at working the derrick, I had no instruction nor on-the-job experience. After a strand or two, I missed the pipe by failing to get the cow's cock locked onto it as the blocks came up. I had pulled the handles but failed to lock the cow's cock shut. The blocks continued upward, and the top of the strand of ninety-foot pipe fell to the opposite side of the derrick. Zeke saw me miss. "Hey, Leon, hold on, I am coming up." The driller lowered the blocks so Zeke could climb on top of the cow's cock. He then raised the blocks back up to the stabbing floor, where Zeke stepped off. It was like riding the most dangerous elevator in the world.

"Leon, you wait here, and I'll go get the pipe. Throw me the end of this rope when I tell you."

Zeke began free climbing around the perimeter of the structure; when he got to the other side, he yelled at me. "Throw me the rope!" I did so, and Zeke wrapped the rope around the pipe and climbed back around the rig to rejoin me on the stabbing floor. We used the rope and pulled the pipe back to the proper position. We moved the top of the pipe to the correct side of the derrick and tied it off. I listened closely to the instructions so I'd know what to do when I would have to do this myself. Zeke gave me a couple of pointers on the technique required to finish the job.

I had been working sixteen hours straight again, and in eight hours, I'd have to be back at work. This meant an hour ride home, a little sleep, a meal, then an hour ride back to the rig. After the shift was over, Zeke and I walked toward the lower doghouse for a beer and to change clothes for the long ride home. Zeke put his arm around my shoulder and began telling me a story.

"Leon, when I started working the derrick years ago, we had a storm come in. It was the middle of the day, and freezing rain just wouldn't quit. We did not have any heat in the derrick. The stabbing floor was glazed over with ice, and I slipped. I had been told to buckle the straps over my shoulders as well as buckle the waist belt on the safety harness. The straps were hurting my shoulders and restricting my movement due to the four layers of clothes I had on. I had unbuckled my shoulder straps but kept the waist belt buckled. When my foot slipped off the stabbing floor, it scared the crap out of me. I thought I was a goner for sure. I was suspended up there six feet below the stabbing floor. Thank God I had the waist belt on. I was safe, as the belt saved me from falling all the way to the drilling floor, but with no shoulder straps and being top heavy, I was hanging upside down about six feet below the stabbing floor. It scared me so bad, hanging upside down eighty-four feet above the drilling floor, I began to pee. As I did, it ran down and into my mouth. At that point, I began throwing up. The crew came up and rescued me, and I vowed I would never work without shoulder straps again."

Although I had laughed at the story, which was funny since Zeke had survived without physical injury, I can't say what effect it had on Zeke's emotional well-being and his sense of pride. At any rate, I took the story seriously. I never wanted to be hanging upside down above the ground. I never worked on the stabbing floor without the waist belt and the shoulder straps buckled.

A few days after, we were driving home, and I was in a bad mood. Earl had put me there. The crew had been working hard again, and again Earl had been slacking off. Everybody was drinking a beer except me.

"Leon, you feel all right? You're awfully quiet, and you're not drinking," Bear asked.

"Sure, I feel okay," I answered.

"Well, you're not drinking. Are you sure everything is okay?" Bear persisted.

I didn't know whether to say anything or keep quiet. I was getting fed up with Earl's attitude. I had always done the job I was asked to do to the best of my ability. I had done this since I was a child. I had also learned that if I didn't do the job and do it right, I would be punished. No, Red was not going to beat me like my father had done, but there would be consequences.

"I decided I don't like drinking with this lazy asshole over here," I said, hooking my thumb toward Earl. About that time, Earl

31

reached over Willie in the back seat of Red's car and poured his beer down my shirt. Startled, I jumped and immediately tried to climb over Willie to get to Earl, but Willie pushed me back into my seat. I glared at Earl.

"All right, asshole, when we stop in Spearman, I'll take care of you!" I snarled at Earl.

Red intervened, "I don't care what y'all do, but you both had better show up for work tomorrow."

The crew arrived in Spearman, and the first stop was to let Earl out near his house. As Earl exited on the passenger side, I bailed out the rear door on the driver's side. Anticipating a fight, Red rolled down his window and yelled above the howl of the wind, "By God, I mean it, you both better be at work tomorrow."

I didn't think about the fact that Red was the boss and should have been dealing with Earl's poor work ethic. I was more focused on the fact that Earl worked so little, and more importantly, that Earl had poured a beer on me.

Well, damn if it hadn't started snowing again! The last snow had melted quickly, so this was all fresh snow. I came around the rear of Red's car and came face to face with Earl. I remembered what my grandfather had taught me about fighting. This lesson had to do with the bully my grandfather had had to deal with when he was sheriff in Keokuk, Iowa, back in the early 1900s. My grandfather had told me that when faced with a bully, to step in and knock the crap out of him. Hit hard, hit fast, hit first. The first shot really counts in this situation.

Wham! I placed the knuckles of my right hand squarely on the left side of Earl's face, and the fight was on! Earl responded with a right hook of his own. Earl outweighed me by a good forty-five to fifty pounds and was a few years older. I was young and skinny but farm-boy strong. I had played basketball and football in high school, and I had speed and agility in my favor.

The intensity of the snow and wind strengthened as our fight escalated. We could hardly see fifty feet in front of us; it was becoming a virtual whiteout. I was wearing my leather-soled cowboy boots and was having a hard time maintaining traction on the fresh snow. I had been slipping around and finally slipped and landed on my ass. Earl jumped on top of me, grabbing me by the throat with both hands and squeezing. I began to panic, then I looked into Earl's eyes. It suddenly dawned on me that those eyes were two really great targets. I placed my thumbs into Earl's eyes and pressed until both thumbs reached the first joint deep into Earl's eye sockets. Earl moved away as quickly as he could, rubbing his eyes. I sprang to my feet, realizing how slippery my boots were in the snow. I got into my best balance and stance and swung my right foot up and into Earl's jaw as he raised up. As Earl went down, I jumped on top as Earl had done to me. I grabbed him by the throat with both hands. I, however, raised Earl's head and slammed it down onto the concrete sidewalk. Red, Bear, and Willie had had a few laughs as they sat in the car, watching the fight and drinking beer. When Red saw what I was doing, he panicked. Watching a couple of guys fight in the middle of a heavy snowstorm was entertaining; however, he didn't want to lose a crew member.

Oh, shit, Leon is going to kill him. Stop him!" All three bailed out of the car, slipping and sliding their way over to us. Willie and Bear grabbed me while Red helped Earl to his feet.

I took a deep breath and relaxed slightly. "Bear, I believe I am ready for that beer now," I said, breathing heavily and sporting a big, shit-eating grin.

"Yes, sir. Let me help you with that," Bear said as he gave me a mock bow. Bear looked at me with a new respect.

While it had been physically and mentally demanding, the fight was over in a matter of minutes. I had been a target for bullies all my life and was now maturing into a man. I never really knew why I had been a bullies' target. It could have been because I was tall and skinny or because of my Mormon religion. All I knew was that I was not about to let anyone push me around, much less pour beer on me. The fight had been an emotional outlet for me. I was no longer in a bad mood. It seemed like eighteen years of being in the Mormon cult and suffering my parents' abuse had all been played out in this fight. I was emotionally drained. The Mormons taught followers to be pacifists and to turn the other cheek. That never worked for me.

Despite the Mormons' teachings, I had grown up with violence. My mother and father had thought nothing of using a backhand, palm, and on one or two occasions they had even used a doubled-up fist to vent their frustration on me. When I was nine, the family car broke down, and the motor had to be overhauled. I worked on this project with my father well into the night. About 2 or 3 a.m., I was still cleaning the old gasket material off the heads on the old V-8 motor. My dad had given me a dull chisel and had ordered me to do this onerous task. I was so exhausted I could hardly hold my arms up or keep my eyes open. My father inspected the cleaning job and erupted in a rage, striking me in the face with his doubled-up fist, rendering me unconscious. As I regained consciousness, I was aware of my father shouting and demanding a better cleaning job. I tried my best, but I was exhausted. Finally, in disgust, my father sent me to the house to bed. After all, I still had to go to school the next morning. My new shiner would be a topic of conversation with the other kids.

But Earl had not been quick or powerful. Crap, my mother, a tall heavy-built woman, slapped me harder than Earl had hit me.

I hardly felt Earl's punches — partly because of fear of losing and partly because of adrenaline coursing through my veins. Delivering a beating to Earl was emotionally the same as beating my father.

We loaded up into Red's Chevrolet Impala as Earl walked off toward his house.

Red continued to drop us, one at a time, at our respective residences. At last Red stopped and let me out.

"I expect you to be at work tomorrow."

"Yes, sir. I'll be ready when you get here."

I went upstairs, and as I opened the door to the hallway that led to the rooms, my landlady happened to be near the top of the stairs and stopped me.

"What the hell happened to you?" she asked with a look of surprise and concern.

"I'm not sure what I look like, but you can bet the other guy looks worse," was all I said.

I was exhausted. I felt like I could sleep for twenty-four hours. I showered, checked my alarm clock, and crawled into bed. I was asleep by the time my head hit the pillow.

The fight had been a huge emotional release for me. Earl was the beneficiary of all the pent-up anger from the years of abuse I'd suffered at the hands of my mother, my father, and fellow Mormon boys. I had also elevated myself in the eyes of the crew.

I made it back to work the next day, but Earl missed three days' work and was in the hospital overnight. Word was, he had cracked or broken ribs. The crew continued to gain respect for me; they quit harassing me and quit threatening to initiate me. They no longer called me Worm.

Days went by, and it got so cold and the relentless wind in the Panhandle was so strong, that some days I really wanted to leave, but I knew I couldn't until my father got better and was out of the hospital. Although it had been three months, based on the last conversation I'd had with my mother, my father was still in the hospital.

Typical winter rig wear in January in the Texas Panhandle consisted of layers: a layer of thermal underwear, a layer of quilted/insulated underwear, denim jeans, a flannel shirt, and then insulated overalls. The crew members typically wore Red Wing insulated steel-toed boots and two layers of socks. Sometimes the wind blew so hard one could not walk directly into the wind and had to tack like a sailboat to get to a position upwind. The work was monotonous, and I generally worked two to three extra shifts a week, so my work week usually landed me around seventy hours' pay. I paid for my essentials, bought groceries and a little beer, and sent the rest home.

My life was a routine of eating, sleeping, and working. My mother never asked about church or what I was doing during my off time, and I never offered any information. I never complained; I just did what I thought I was supposed to do — except for the drinking and fighting. Hell, these were two of the most important activities of oil field trash. I was fine-tuning my drinking skills and working on my fighting skills. Nobody ever gave me any shit, and that's what I wanted. I didn't care all that much for human interaction; I had grown up with a bunch of Holstein cattle and a couple of dogs. I felt comfortable that, as the oldest male in the family who could work, I was fulfilling my responsibilities. My brother was twelve years younger, not old enough to work, and he was the apple of our father's eye. Though I had not felt love or acceptance from my parents at any time during my life, my family was still the only family I had, and I was always trying to gain their acceptance. My parents saw me as just a workhorse and someone to vent their anger and frustration on.

Toward the end of the winter, a blizzard hit while we were at the rig. Red spun into action. "Bear and Willie, I want you to put up more tarps," he directed. "There is a storm coming. The drill bit is dull. Leon and Earl, we need to pull the pipe out of the hole. Get everything ready."

Five hours later, disaster hit!

I was suddenly struck with severe abdominal cramps and was feeling dizzy and lightheaded.

Doubled over, holding my stomach, I said to Red, "I'm dizzy and feeling sick to my stomach."

"Me, too. I'm calling the tool pusher." As Red said this, my legs turned to rubber, and I watched the world around me spin out of control. I was unable to stop my fall as I passed out on the drill floor. Unknowingly, Earl, Willie, Red, and I had been breathing exhaust fumes while working downwind of the big diesel motors on the drilling floor. The two V-12 diesel engines had been working hard running the rig, while we were working in blizzard conditions. Sometime during the shift, the wind had changed direction and had blown the exhaust fumes over to and down onto the drilling floor. Bear was in the derrick, so he had not been affected, but when he saw me go down, he immediately took off his harness and made the ninety-foot trip down the pipe to the drill floor. Red called the tool pusher over the two-way radio and used the word *"emergency."* The tool pusher came. The workers who had been affected by the carbon monoxide gasses —Willie, Earl, and Red, and I — were loaded into the tool pusher's car and into Bear's car and driven to Perryton General Hospital in Perryton, Texas, the closest care center. I had not regained consciousness and was in a coma when I reached the hospital. Earl, Red, and Willie were checked at the hospital and released. I woke up three days later.

"Where am I?" I asked groggily.

"You are at the hospital in Perryton," a voice answered.

"What happened? Was there an accident?" I asked.

"Yes, you have had carbon monoxide poisoning. You have been in a coma for three days," came the reply.

The medical staff explained to me what had happened and that I was now determined to be in good health and could return to work if I was ready. I was ready. The tool pusher showed up that afternoon to drive me back to Spearman. He told me that he had heard about the fight between Earl and me and said that Earl had needed a good butt kickin'.

"You have had it rough the last few days. I thought we were going to lose you. Are you ready to go home?" the tool pusher asked.

"Yes, sir, I'll get changed," I answered. I felt good, albeit still a little weak. As we drove, the tool pusher again mentioned the fight. He told me that the company was considering me for a promotion.

When I got home to my room, I wrote a letter to my mom. I chose to communicate by mail since phone calls were too expensive. My mother occasionally wrote back, but her letters said nothing to clue me in on crucial information: She had developed a drug dependency, and she was getting worse. I did know that she had had numerous ailments over the years and had visited different doctors numerous times. It seemed that the preferred and most common drugs the doctors prescribed for her were valium and opiates. Later, I would learn more about her conditions, but for the time being I was focused on taking care of my family. No one but the drilling company and the hospital knew of my condition that week. I never told my parents of my brush with death. I didn't think it would really matter to them other than that I had lost three days of work, and the money order I sent home would be substantially less.

As Red pulled up in front of my apartment the next morning, he was elated to see me waiting for him.

"Damn, it's good to see you! How are you doing? Are you ready to go to work?"

"Hell, yes, I have had enough of hospitals and doctors for a while. Let's go."

I climbed into Red's car, while Bear, Willie, and Earl joked and teased me. These men felt like family. They were there when you needed them. We didn't always get along, but we cared about each other. I was touched by the concern in their voices when they asked how I was doing. I felt they genuinely wanted to know.

The work routine and schedule quickly got back to normal. My nineteenth birthday was coming up, and I couldn't have suspected what the crew had cooked up for me. No one had leaked a word. Toward the end of November as we were headed to the rig one night, Red made his usual stop at the liquor store.

"I want some whiskey tonight," Bear said. "Yes, me too," Willie chimed in. "Leon, what are you having?"

I asked for my usual beer. That was all I wanted and all I ever drank.

We got to the rig. I took the geological samples; the bit was running smoothly, and it was colder than hell outside, so we started popping a few tops in the lower doghouse. Midnight rolled around, and it was time for us to take off to go home. Everybody loaded into Red's car. After drinking for the best part of eight hours, we were pretty well hammered, especially me. I was sober enough to notice, however, that we were going in a different direction from home.

"Hey, where are we going?"

Bear responded, "I know a very special place over in Guymon. That's where we are heading."

"What place?"

"You'll find out soon enough." Red said with a silly grin.

I was a little confused but was too busy drinking to care. We had been drilling close to the panhandle of Oklahoma, and Guymon, Oklahoma, was not far away. Before long, we pulled up to a reasonably nice hotel in Guymon, and the guys surprised me by singing *Happy Birthday*. I was a little curious about why we had stopped at a hotel, but the crew was too busy laughing and acting sly to say. We all got out, and the crew, led by Bear, escorted me into the hotel and up the stairs where Bear knocked on a door. An attractive brunette in her early thirties opened the door; she was wearing nothing but a red, sheer negligee. I had a hard time taking my eyes off her. Every time I looked away, my eyes drifted back to her flat stomach, large breasts, and shapely hips. Bear spoke with her for a moment, gave her something, then introduced her to me.

I was grinning from ear to ear but managed to say, "Hey."

The brunette took my arm and ushered me inside. Bear held his arms out to block the other guys from entering the room. They were laughing and cracking crude jokes. I paid no attention to them. My focus was entirely on this sparsely dressed female.

"Come on, guys. Let's head back down to the car," Bear suggested.

"Oh, come on. Why can't we stay?"

"Well, you can sit here in the hallway, or you can sit in the car and have another beer. Choice is yours," Bear said as he turned and walked down the hallway.

The woman quickly surmised the situation: I was still a virgin and was drunk on my ass to boot.

We stood there, assessing each other. My head was spinning — and not from the beer. Wow! She was good looking. She was tall and lean. She was almost as tall as I was. She was wearing a red, sheer, sexy, little one-piece that lifts the breasts up — not that she needed any help. She had on sheer black nylons and a black garter belt. I might have been drunk, but that didn't prevent my soldier from standing tall.

"Leon, would you like to take your clothes off?"

"Huh?"

She started unsnapping my pearl-button cowboy shirt.

"Let's take these off, too," she murmured as she unzipped my jeans.

I felt awkward and embarrassed, standing there in only my skivvies. Standing back from me, so I could see her, she slipped her right finger under the strap on her left shoulder. She slowly slid the thin strap down to her elbow. She then slowly slid the strap from her right arm. She reached up with both hands and slowly slid her sheer red negligee and her hands over her breasts and down her flat stomach, ending in a V at the vortex between her legs.

I hadn't had any experience with women and wasn't sure what to do, but I immediately forgot about my embarrassment. She was in charge, especially since I was so inexperienced and had been drinking. I obeyed her commands. My head was swirling. I had never seen a woman without clothes before, and I was dealing with the effects of the alcohol. We wrapped up our activity, and the woman escorted me out of the room. I made my way downstairs where the crew was waiting. When they caught sight of me, they started hollerin', yellin', whistling, and laughing. Bear was laughing so hard he had water squirting out of his eyes. What a bunch of great guys, I thought. Although Earl hadn't participated, I was elated that the crew had thought so much of me that they gave me this very special birthday surprise. The madame had been patient, gentle like a woman can be, and respectful with me. I had learned a great deal from her regarding a woman's body. I would always remember her warmly. Still a lit-tle embarrassed, I thanked each guy individually. So much for the Mormon way of life now, I thought. I had become a drinker and a fornicator. This was a hell of a lot more fun than reading the Bible, the Book of Mormon, and praying all the time. From what I knew, Mormons were judgmental and condemning of anyone who did not follow their ways. If they were to find out about this activity, I would certainly be excommunicated. I rarely met any Mormons I liked. I did tolerate them, but I genuinely liked these oilfield guys.

Thinking of how much I liked my crew brought to mind two Mormon boys I particularly disliked. The boys were the sons of the Mormon bishop. The bishop tried to toughen up his sons by beating them. In turn, they would beat up me, a twelve-year-old, at church. One Sunday before services began, Rick, who was sixteen, and Randy, who was eighteen, were wearing my ass out when I attempted to get away by running around a bush to get around the corner of the building, into the bathroom, and lock the door. Dean, fourteen years old and the third attacker, was on my heels and followed me into the bathroom before I could get the door closed and locked. Dean was not related to the bishop, but seeing Rick and Randy chase and beat up on me, he thought it looked like fun, so he chased me into the bathroom. Although Dean was two years older, I had worked on a farm as a kid, moving hay, feed, and buckets of milk; I was plenty strong. As Dean approached me, I got him off balance enough to push him into the bathroom stall. Dean quit having so much fun when he began blowing bubbles into the bottom of the commode and gasping for air. Soon thereafter, the beatings ceased. Someone must have told the bishop what shitheads his two sons were and what they had been doing. So much for brothers in Mormonism! What a shithead the bishop must have been to raise two sons like that. The abuse I suffered at their hands affected me for many years.

The Christmas holiday was soon upon us, and I continued to be a dependable, hardworking young man. On Christmas day, I stood as usual on the sidewalk waiting for Red, the temperature was unusually warm as the sun was shining.

"Merry Christmas, Leon," Red called out of his open window as he drove up to my apartment.

"Merry Christmas, everybody," I responded as I climbed into the back seat.

As usual we stopped at the liquor store, but it was closed for the holiday. Bear and Willie went around back to the owner's apartment and asked him to open it for us. The owner was happy to open the store for his faithful, regular, and frequent customers, and we prepared for Christmas on the rig. We bought lots of beer and some bourbon. When we got to the rig, we found that the earlier shift crew had everything running like a well-oiled machine. Bear checked the items in his normal routine; Willie checked the motors, and I collected ore samples from the pit. We sang a Christmas song or two while we drank our beverages, and as had happened before, we were drunk by the time the shift was over. Still, we made it back to Spearman. Red dropped off everyone except me. I had gotten out of Red's car with Bear. Bear had invited me to go with him to Borger, Texas, to see the biggest drilling rig in Texas and to pick up Bear's sister. The rig looked much like the one we had been working on but was a lot bigger. This rig could drill up to 10,000 feet.

After finding the rig and sightseeing, we went to a bar and pizza place where Bear's sister worked. We spent a little time at the pizza parlor and had a beer, then piled into Bear's car and, bringing his sister along, we began the trip back to Spearman.

"Leon, can you drive for a while?" Bear asked drowsily.

"Sure, no problem," I said, but I also had been up all day and nearly all night and had been drinking a lot.

It was well into the night, and I had been driving for a while and was still drinking beer. I realized I must have taken a wrong turn. I was on a dirt road in the middle of nowhere in the middle of the night. I stopped the car and looked around, but there were no road signs, no pavement, just what looked like an endless desert. When I came to a stop, Bear woke up and got out of the car. He also looked around.

"Where the hell are we?"

"Sorry, Bear, I must have taken a wrong turn. I have absolutely no idea where we are," I confessed.

"Since we are stopped, I need to stretch my legs." Bear yawned and took a step forward.

"Holy shit, Leon, look!"

I stepped up next to Bear and looked down. Less than thirty feet in front of the car was a sheer cliff drop. The bottom of the canyon was not visible in the dark. If I had not stopped where I had, the three of us would have found out exactly where the bottom of the canyon was.

"What the hell? Is that Palo Duro Canyon?" I asked.

"It must be, or another big son of a bitch just like it. One more minute and we would have been down there!" Bear pointed to the bottom of the deep canyon.

That sobered both of us up. Bear's sister had slept through the entire trip and was not aware that I had almost killed all three of us.

Bear said, "Let's get going, I'll drive."

"Be my guest."

We managed to make it back to Spearman in one piece. At 2:30 that afternoon I was still hungover and had had very little sleep but was ready and waiting on the sidewalk for Red to pick me up. I waited for some time, but Red didn't show up. I walked up the street to the local telephone booth and dialed Red's number.

"Hello, Red?"

"Yes, this is Red."

"Are we working today?" I asked.

"No, I will not be picking you up today." Apparently, even Red had gotten so drunk he could not make it to work.

It happened to be a beautiful, sunny but cool day, so I decided to get my Honda 305 Scrambler out for a spin. I rode it around for a little while then stopped at a telephone booth. I had decided to call my mother and wanted to wish her and my younger brother and sister a Merry Christmas.

"Merry Christmas!" I said cheerfully.

"Merry Christmas, Leon. Did you send this week's money? It should have been in the mail yesterday."

"Mom, I sent it a couple of days ago. You should get it soon."

"We better. I have mouths to feed, and your father still isn't able to work."

"How is he doing?"

"He is recovering and should be able to return to work in a couple of months."

"How are you?"

"I am as well as can be expected. I got through giving birth to you. You were huge — nine pounds, ten ounces. I have never been the same since. Damn, you almost killed me."

I had heard this repeatedly throughout my life. My mother frequently found a way to blame me for her physical and mental difficulties. If she tripped on the corner of a rug, she would tell me it was because I had weakened her legs when I was born.

I tried to change the subject. "How are the kids?"

"They are good. I caught your sister in the garage kissing the boy from next door. I had to send her to her room to think about the Book of Mormon and the Bible. She's young and curious."

Dang, I thought. If I had been caught doing something that I wasn't supposed to do, I would get a backhand or possibly even knocked unconscious. I thought again about how my parents had treated me, using angry words and physical violence. Was it something I had done? I had rationalized that maybe I had been adopted or was the result of an illicit affair and was resented by both my parents through no fault of my own.

Still on the phone, I saw a Big Bear Yamaha motorcycle come buzzing by. The rider turned his head and looked at my Honda. A minute or two later I could hear the rider winding up that two-cycle motor, and he was coming fast! Showing off. As the bike and rider neared the intersection traveling south, a station wagon driven by a woman going north turned left into the intersection; the bike was coming into the intersection from the opposite way at a high rate of speed. When the woman in the station wagon turned left, the rider had to lean to his left to avoid the station wagon, which was now directly in front of him. In the meantime, the black car behind the station wagon swerved right to go around the station wagon and met the rider and bike head on. The Yamaha was swept under the black car, which was driven by an old man, and the motorcycle rider, on impact, went straight up into the air; he did a one-and-a-half twist and a forward somersault before landing on his head on the pavement.

"What's going on? What's all that noise?" My mother could hear the crash over the telephone line.

46

"Mom, you would not believe this." I described the action and scene. "There was a motorcycle accident right in front of me, and I think the rider has been killed."

"That's terrible. Leon; you be careful."

I thought this might be a good time to end the call before my mother started talking about the dangers of riding and or sharing any other negative thoughts about me that might be passing through her mind.

"Okay, Mom, I hope to see you soon. Tell everybody I said hello and Merry Christmas."

I saw in the newspaper the following day that, sure enough, the rider had been killed. Witnessing the accident and having seen someone killed had freaked me out. I put the bike back in storage and left it there. I didn't know if I would ever ride it again.

A few days later, the crew loaded up, and Red chauffeured us as usual, stopping at the liquor store on the way to the rig. The temperature was about twenty degrees, as it often was below freezing in the Texas Panhandle in the winter, and the wind was blowing about twenty-five to thirty mph, again, as usual. The crew got to the rig, and Willie checked the oil levels on the Waukeshas, checked the grease, and basically made his first rounds. I collected a pouch and headed downstairs to get my first soil sample of the night. Bear and Earl checked tarps and supplies. The evening set in early in the winter, and it got dark around 6 p.m. The Waukeshas were running smoothly like a pair of giant sewing machines. I had nothing to do but retrieve samples every hour, but there was a small issue. I collected the first sample and went up to the driller's doghouse.

"Red, I have a rash on my wrists, and it hurts pretty bad."

"Let me see your wrists," Red instructed.

I pushed my sleeves up a little so Red could see what I was referring to.

"Holy crap, Leon, how long has this been this way?" Red sounded worried. I told him, for a couple of days.

I had to put my forearms into the pit to obtain the samples. This pit was full of water and chemicals from the water that is forced down through the drill pipe into the hole. It would force mud to rise into the pit. This soil was used for testing by the geologists. From the relentless, fierce, freezing winds, getting my wrists wet eight times every night, and the chemicals in the mud, my wrists were red, rough, and nearly raw.

"Leon, here are seven more bags. Label them for the night samples, staggering the times by one hour. Then go get seven more samples and come back here," Red ordered. I filled out the labels, then went downstairs and filled the seven other bags with ore samples from the pit.

I then took the full sample bags and put them in the sample box for the geologists.

Red handed me a bottle of liquid. "Here's some lotion. Put this on your wrists a few times tonight. Maybe by tomorrow they will be better." Red was hopeful.

The next day Red approached me and asked to see my wrists.

"I think they're doing much better," I said. I, too, was hopeful.

"Put this lotion on before you take ore samples out of the pit," Red advised. I followed his advice, and there were no more problems with the rash after that.

With the rig running smoothly, I went out to the pile of rice hulls. The hulls were packaged in large burlap bags and would be dumped into the circulation pit when the gauges indicated the pressure was low. The graph and charts, as well as pressure gauges, kept the crew informed of the status of the bit. I decided to move a few of the bags of the rice hulls around to build a parapet wall around the perimeter of the bags, with a sunken area in the middle of the stack. In effect, I had hollowed out a space big enough to allow me to lie down on my back, be blocked from the direct wind, and look at the stars. I had done this from time to time to give my mind some rest and find some peace, as so many things that had happened in my short life did not make sense. This was the beginning of my searching for peace. I would study meditation a few years later.

I had learned that the men I had been working with were kind, caring, and honest people. I felt that they were more honest and more sincere than the pretentious churchgoers and Bible-worshippers I had grown up around. I had learned in a very short time to trust the men I had worked with in Spearman, while the Mormons always seemed to have some agenda, and I have found that many were not trustworthy. I was, without being aware of it, looking for peace. Life at home always involved lots of drama.

My father was healing, and I figured I would soon be going back home. Even though I had always felt I was different, was blamed for everything that went wrong, and was frequently struck by my mother or father, I did miss my family, and the life I'd led was the only life I knew.

I was having conflicting feelings and did not understand the psychology behind my feelings. I was happy to have stepped up and helped out my father and mother and to have helped feed my younger brother and sister. My older sister had gotten married and had moved into a house a few blocks from our parents' house. I had been forced to grow up overnight by going to the oil fields. This I did willingly and proudly, but I wasn't too sure about going home. At home I was a

Mormon; here I was oil field trash, just another beer-drinking, fighting roughneck. The two worlds were 180 degrees apart.

The oil derrick where I went to work
as a naïve 18-year-old.

CHAPTER 2

Going Home

I'd gotten a letter from Mother telling me that Dad had been released from the hospital and was working again. I could quit my job and go home. I was conflicted about going home. I had kept my rent payments up and had kept my apartment reasonably clean. My standing at Baker and Taylor was excellent. Ultimately, I decided to tell everyone I'd be leaving and gave a week's notice to Red. Even though I had qualms about returning to the Mormon religion and lifestyle, going home seemed to be the right thing to do. After all, I did love my family, and I missed them. I would be returning to what was most familiar to me.

The week flew by, but I was ready. The crew bid me goodbye. I paid my storage bill, picked up my Honda Scrambler, stuffed it into the trunk of my Chevy Super Sport, and headed back to Missouri and my family.

When I got home, my family treated me like I was a stranger. I couldn't make sense of this since I had been away only to work to support the people who were now treating me so strangely. I tried to figure out what I might have done to offend, but I couldn't come up with an answer. True enough, I hadn't been following the Mormon lifestyle, but I had put my life on hold and at risk to help my family.

Before long, my father approached me: "Leon, something has really been bothering me. While you were in the oil fields, you did not attend church! Ever!" he growled.

"That's right," I confessed.

"And you haven't attended since you have returned from the oil fields?" he challenged.

"That's right, too."

"Do you plan on returning to the church?" he asked.

"I'm not interested in going to church right now," I gave an honest reply.

"*Get out of my house!*" he screamed and stood stiffly at his full five feet, eight inches, extending his arm, pointing to the front door.

I looked at my father as I stood to leave the room. I didn't want to start another conflict with my dad. I now was much taller and stronger than he was. I didn't want to hurt my father, so I chose to walk away.

I'd always felt different from the rest of my family, and I felt out of place more so now than ever. My mother suggested that I move in with my older sister, Ilene. Her husband was an over-the-road trucker, and if I moved in with her, she would have someone there at night with her. So, I moved in with Ilene and got a job at a local manufacturing company, making about half or less than what I had been making in the oil field. But it wasn't too awfully bad, as I did not have to share my income with anyone else or pay any rent. My sister bought all the food. Nevertheless, I was barely making enough to pay my expenses. I drove my Honda around town in my free time, as it was one of the few things I enjoyed doing, and it gave me a sense of freedom.

On one of these rides, I met another motorcyclist, Johnny Whitehorse. Whitehorse rode the coolest bike I had ever seen. It was a 1947 Knucklehead manufactured by Harley Davidson. Whitehorse had stripped a lot of the factory parts off, extended the front end, and trimmed down the full-dress Harley, making it into what was called in that day a "Chopper."

About this time, the Hell's Angels biker group in California and Arizona was in its heyday, and they were making news. Sonny Barger, the organization's president, had just published a book. I was drawn to the idea of biking. In a struggle to find myself, find some peace of mind and my place in this new society, I started hanging out with Whitehorse and a few other bikers, and before long, Whitehorse told me that he knew of an old Harley for sale. I was beside myself; this was something I really wanted. I had managed to save a few dollars from my oil field earnings, although it wasn't much, as I had sent home pretty much everything I had been paid. I had also sold my 305 Honda Scrambler. Whitehorse set up the meeting, and he and I drove over to look at the old Harley.

Johnny Whitehorse introduced himself to the bike's owner. "I spoke with you on the phone a couple of days ago. We came over to look at an old Harley Panhead for sale."

"It's over here in the barn," the man said.

Walking toward the garage, I could feel my excitement rising. The possibility of having my own Harley — wow!

We entered a large hay barn and began to move loose and baled hay from around the Harley. The bike was a Duo-Glide that had been introduced by Harley Davidson in 1949.

From 1936 to 1947, Harley made a Knucklehead with a springer front end. In 1948, Harley changed the design of the motor, and the newly designed motor was called a Panhead. In 1948, Harley kept the springer front end and replaced the Knucklehead motor with the new and improved Panhead. Then in 1949, Harley installed a Panhead motor and a new-style front end. This bike was made during the first year of the new front end and was complete with closed-in tubing and front shocks. Initially, I saw that the bike was pretty much factory stock. However, it had chrome split tanks, which were not stock. I thought the huge gas tank and bulky front end were butt-ugly, but it was a Harley.

Whitehorse asked the owner if it would start. The owner checked the oil, fetched a gas can, and we rolled the bike out of the barn. The owner kicked the bike a few times, added some fresh gasoline, and the bike started. I had never heard better music. I loved the sound of Whitehorse's bike with drag pipes; this one had factory exhausts, but it still had that Harley rumble, and it was music to my ears.

"How much do you want for it?" asked Whitehorse.

"$125," responded the farmer.

I looked at Whitehorse. "What do you think?"

"Leon, this is the only old Harley for sale that I know of, and I think the price is okay."

I turned to the farmer. "Who do I make the check out to?"

I paid the seller. Whitehorse got into his car, and I straddled my Harley and started it again. I knew my sister's garage didn't have enough room for me to work on my new motorcycle. We drove instead to my parents' house some fifteen miles away. My parents seldom had anything in their garage. I parked the old Harley in the run-down, detached garage and closed the doors.

"Whitehorse, you're going to help me work on this, aren't you, because I don't know anything about a Harley." I beseeched my friend.

"No problem. I'll be over after work tomorrow, and we'll get started. I know where there are some used parts you can use to make your bike look really cool."

Whitehorse was enthusiastic about the project, and I was ready to get started.

Not surprisingly, my mother asked me about the Harley and wanted to know where I got the money to buy it. She wanted to know if I had any more money I could donate to the family. I explained that I had saved a little and that what I had left wasn't much, and I would need to buy parts.

My father didn't like having an evil machine in his garage, but for some reason, which remains a mystery to me, my father left me alone when I was working on my motorcycle.

I didn't have much cash left, so I couldn't afford to buy new or premium parts. Eventually, we found a '48 springer front end with a Harley 165 front wheel and tire. I bought it and a Harley 165 teardrop gas tank. We found a bobbed rear fender and sixteen-inch ape hanger handlebars, too. I had to get a new throttle cable, a small leather solo seat, and an ignition switch as well, because there were no used ones to be found. The throttle cable's length was unique to fit the ape hangers and handlebar risers. I'd have to make a road trip to buy this. The closest Harley dealership was in Springfield, Missouri, more than seventy miles away. Three of my friends and I made the trip in my '62 Impala Super Sport.

I pulled up to a large, brick warehouse and walked past new and used Harleys lined up outside the entrance. My eyes were jumping from one bike to another. Man, I loved Harleys — their lines and sounds were beautiful to me. This was the first Harley dealership I had been in, and I really wanted to soak it all in. I wandered around the shop floor looking at bikes, clothes, and parts. Some of the customers looked a little rough, but I was used to rough-cut folks; I felt an immediate bond, like I belonged. I was building a custom bike for myself, and with Whitehorse's help, I was up to the task.

I bought a Harley owner's manual along with a new switch that contained an electrical wiring diagram. Since I had stripped all those things off that I had considered to be non-essentials, I had to interpret the factory wiring diagram and install the wiring to fit my custom Chopper. Whitehorse was there all along to assist. Whitehorse knew a lot, but this was a custom build, and there were quite a few things that required custom engineering and tweaking.

Whitehorse and I got it running, and I had begun to ride my Harley around town (I had sold the Honda Scrambler to buy parts for my HOG) with Whitehorse and our friends, Butch and Clancy. Clancy usually had his girlfriend with him, but the rest of us rode solo. None of us were bad asses, but we were not to be messed with, either. It seemed as though everybody accepted that, and there was no violence. Some of us wore leather jackets with a denim vest that had been fashioned from a jacket. Although I didn't act in a threatening way, when I would go into a grocery store, strangers would get out of the aisle as I entered. The police harassed us a little here and there because of our long hair, beards, bikes, and clothes. But sometimes, people who judged us by our looks were quick to jump to the wrong conclusion.

One afternoon, Butch, Wolf, Whitehorse, and I rode down to the river on the south side of town. The riverbed was solid rock, and the water was only a few inches deep just above the falls. It was so shallow that people would sometimes drive their cars onto the rocks to wash their cars in the river. This was the case with a tall, slender brunette we saw that day. We were drinking a little beer and watching people at the edge of the river when the girl drove up and got out of her car. I had to look twice to see if she was wearing anything, as her bikini top and bottom were skimpy, to say the least. She got out of her car with a rag and began rubbing the car down. She leaned over the hood of the car, exposing breasts barely covered by a small triangle of cloth. She extended her shapely butt outward. It looked to me like she wanted some attention, so I figured I would give her some. At the encouragement of my friends, I got up and began moving toward her.

I spoke to her: "Good afternoon."

"Afternoon," she replied.

"Beautiful day," I said, smiling, as I placed my hand on her upper arm.

"What do you think you are doing?" she demanded, as she swung around and slapped me in the face with her wet rag.

My eyes widened, and I jerked back as the wet rag struck me.

"Oh, sorry," I said as I turned around and began making my way back to my friends. They were laughing heartily and razzing me. I thought it was funny too; after all, no harm, no foul.

We spent another hour hanging out, laughing, and drinking. The guys ribbed me about my slap in the face. I had meant no harm and did nothing more aggressive than touch her upper arm.

When the day was done, Wolf and I were riding home — me to my parents' house to put up my bike, and Wolf to his own place. Hearing sirens approaching, we pulled over to let the emergency vehicle pass. We stopped and got off our Harleys.

A police car pulled up behind us and stopped. An officer got out and approached me.

"What's up, Officer? I asked.

"We have had an attempted rape charge filed, and you fit the description of the attacker."

"What did I do, Officer?" I asked.

"Where were you about ninety minutes ago?"

"We were down at the river."

"What did you do at the river?"

"We were just having a couple of beers, swimming, and having a good time."

"Put your hands behind your back," the officer demanded. "The charge is attempted rape."

"You're kidding, right? I'm being arrested… for rape?" I felt dizzy and was barely able to catch myself before I fell. I had actually had quite a few beers and was most certainly drunk. I wondered what the hell the brunette had told the police.

"For attempted rape." The officer repeated.

We were in the alley two doors down from my parents' house.

"Officer, can I put my bike in there? That's my parents' house," I asked.

Wolf reassured him. "Don't worry about it, Leon. I got your bike; go with them.

The officer read me my rights, put me into the back seat of the police car, and we drove to the police station. I was fingerprinted, photographed, and put into a jail cell. A million things were going through my mind: how the heck did I get arrested for attempted rape? I had only touched her upper arm. What had I done to cause this? What was I going to do now? Who should I call? I couldn't call my parents because their phone had been disconnected for non-payment, again. I didn't call anyone. I was tired and decided to sleep and figure it out the next morning.

When we had gone to the river, we had taken a dip to cool off, and my clothes were still wet. Wearing wet clothes in an air-conditioned building caused me to shiver most of the night. I had not been given a mattress or blanket and had to lie on a cold, steel bunk.

Morning came, and I got a surprise.

"Hey Leon, Wolf told me you had a little problem. Are you ready to get out of here?" It was Dalton, a friend from work who was also a Harley owner.

"Hey Dalton, you asshole, what the hell are you doing here? Can't say I'm sorry to see you."

"I told Timmy to give me his keys, and I rode his Honda down here to get you out, you knucklehead. We took up a collection at work for the bail money. Just about everybody donated."

I went through the release process. I retrieved my wallet and keys and went outside with Dalton, who had brought a couple of kids' plastic helmets so we would look as if we were complying with helmet laws. One looked like a football helmet, and the other looked like a WWII German Nazi helmet. I complained that the helmet was too small for my head, but we put them on the best we could.

When we walked outside, I saw sitting in all its glory: a Red Honda 90cc. Our Harleys were 1,200 ccs. So now, here we were, two Harley bikers: Dalton, a tall, husky, well-known double throw-down badass built like an NFL linebacker; and tall, lanky me. All anyone had to do was say fight to Dalton, and he would say, "Where? I want in." Dalton was known to go to nearby towns and bars looking for the most badass guy around, find him, and then proceed to kick his ass. But today, rough-and-tough Dalton and I, two big young men, climbed onto a little bitty Honda 90 and rode down Main Street with children's plastic helmets sitting atop our heads. We must have looked like the proverbial "two monkeys on a football." With me riding on the passenger seat behind Dalton, he took me to the plant where we worked. The Honda's small tires were nearly flat from carrying our combined weight of 400-plus pounds.

I greeted my friends. "Hey, y'all, how are you doing? Thanks for getting me out. Wish I'd gotten a photo."

Timmy, who owned the Honda we'd ridden back on, laughed, "You guys look like Alley Oop and Spiderman riding on a scooter."

"Up yours," I laughed.

I had been arrested, booked into jail and had gotten out before my family ever heard any of the story.

Dalton had a Harley also, but it was parked at his house, and he had ridden to work with Damon, his older brother. That was why he had used Timmy's Honda 90cc to pick me up. Damon was not only older than Dalton but was bigger and stronger as well. He had a reputation for being the absolute baddest badass of all the badasses around the tri- state area. He was built like an NFL nose tackle.

Dalton had been having some issues with the wiring on his Harley. He was extremely frustrated, as he had paid two different motorcycle shops to work on the wiring, but the lights still did not work correctly. When he found out that I had wired my own bike, he asked me to look at the wiring on his. I agreed to do this. I took my trusty Harley owner's manual to use as a reference guide in working on Dalton's bike. When I showed up to help, Damon asked what the hell I was doing there.

"Leave him alone, Damon; he's going to try to fix my wiring," Dalton explained.

"Bullshit, he's no mechanic. If two different shops have failed to fix your wiring, how the hell is he going to do it?" challenged Damon.

"Leave him alone, Damon," countered Dalton.

I didn't join in on the conversation. I just got out my manual and referred to it as I began tracing wires. After making a couple of wiring changes in relatively short order, I turned the switch, and the lights came on as they should have. Dalton straddled his bike, turned the switch on, and kicked it through. It started on his second try.

Dalton's bike was now running, lights working, and with a shit-eating grin, he looked at me. Then, still grinning, he looked at Damon.

"Thumbs up, asshole. I knew you could do it. How now, Damon?" Damon grunted and shot us the finger as he stalked off without saying a word.

Dalton was jubilant. Nobody better mess with me now! Dalton came from the school of "I got your back, brother." I liked helping others. I had supported my family, always carried my load and then some on the rig, and now I was helping my biker friends.

My life had gone from living as a Mormon to being bona-fide oil field trash, and now I was a biker. I was slowly moving up in society.

I went to visit my family. I greeted my mother, father, and younger brother.

"How have you been?" I asked Dad.

"I've been good. I've been hauling loads over the highways. Gone much of the time."

"How've you been, Mom?"

"Oh, you know. My lower back and shoulders are bothering me. I had to increase my pain pills. You know this is because I gave you life." Mother spat at me and walked from the room.

"So, how have you been, Leon?" my brother asked.

"I've been good — really busy at work. I've been a little tired." I decided not to announce the news of my recent arrest.

As I was leaving, my father spoke: "Leon, I have something for you; wait here." I was curious because my parents never gave me anything. In fact, they were usually stealing from me.

Dad brought out a small, dark green glass bottle with no label. It was the size and shape of a typical prescription bottle, and it contained about twenty-five black capsules.

"You know what to do with this," he said, handing me the bottle. I placed the bottle into my pocket, saying nothing. I had no idea what my father had given me. I had never taken pills or even smoked pot. I didn't even know what kind of pills they were. I wasn't overly concerned about them because all my life, I had seen both my mother and father take pills.

I went out that night with Dalton, some other biker friends, and a skinny blonde who had started hanging with us. I showed them the bottle.

Bart, a biker friend, examined the contents of the bottle and said, "Leon, these are RJS Black Mollies from Mexico. Holy shit! They are each 50 milligrams of some really strong amphetamines. Where did you get them?"

"My dad. So, do you know what they are or what they do?" I knew nothing about amphetamines.

"Not sure," Bart confessed. "Let's take one and find out."

I shrugged. Surely, my father wouldn't have given me pills that could hurt me. I didn't know that these pills are the very reason he had a heart attack and was put into the hospital. I gave one to each of my friends, and I took one. Shortly thereafter, I began to feel energized, like I could run a marathon.

"Hey, man, are you guys ready to ride?" I asked.

"Sure, let's go," said Bart.

We climbed onto our bikes, the blonde getting on behind Bart, and off we went. The wind in my face made me feel free and in tune with the universe. It also made me feel cool. We rode for a while.

Next morning at the plant, Dalton asked me whether I'd slept the night before.

"Not a wink," I said. "So, do you want another pill before we start work?"

"Yes, give me another one," Dalton said.

Work started at 7 a.m., and by 11 a.m. both Dalton and I had completed our quota for the day. It usually took us until somewhere between 1 and 3 p.m. to finish, but we were so wired we were in hyper mode. Thank God, the factory had a game room with a ping pong table. For the next four hours, Dalton and I wore out the ping pong balls and paddles. Later that night, we saw the blonde and Bart. The blonde said she hadn't felt anything unusual but that she had not slept, either. She wanted another pill, but both Bart and I chose to not take another, as we both wanted to sleep.

My father had been and still was an over-the-road trucker. He had apparently been taking amphetamines to stay awake and be able to drive more miles per day. Dad got paid by the mile, and more miles equaled a bigger paycheck. But it was the abuse of those little black pills that had put him into the hospital the year before. Maybe I should have noticed that Dad was abusing drugs. But it was hard to tell whether Dad was acting strange, as he had always been a little goofy. His constantly moving our family around illustrated his instability. He was always changing jobs: truck driver, dairy farmer, doing whatever he could find to do. My father even once admitted to me that his own brothers and sisters had nicknamed him "Goofy" when he was a kid.

Thank God that my grandfather Hank, on my mother's side, had lived with us for a while and taught me a lot. My parents taught me only what was needed for me to help my father work. My grandfather taught me to shoot a rifle, hunt, and fish. My grandfather and I would sit and talk whenever we could. Hank also taught me a few of life's philosophies. Despite my grandfather's influence, I was a mixed-up, emotional kid who was the size of a full-grown man.

When I was an adolescent on the farm, I remember my father being so goofy that he would trick me and then laugh. My father would tell me that he had turned off the power to the electric fence. I would walk over to cross the fence, put my hand on the wire, and get the crap shocked out of me. My father would laugh and laugh. As a result of this and other tricks, I never really trusted my father. When I was about fourteen, my dad was home from his trucking job one weekend. The night before, I had heard an extremely heated argument between Dad and Mom. This wasn't unusual, and I just tried to ignore it. The next day, I was outside near the little barn when my father approached me.

"Leon, come over here; I want to show you something." Dad pulled out a pair of dice, knelt down on his knees, and looked at me. "This is how you play craps," he said, and began explaining the game of chance. He rolled the two dice. I felt extremely uncomfortable seeing the look and excitement in my dad's eyes and the way he handled the dice. It was obvious, even to me, a teenager, that my father was a gambler and was very familiar with this game. I realized my father had a gambling problem, and that was what he and Mom had probably been arguing about. This helped me understand why I had gone to bed hungry so many nights. My father was a devoted Mormon, Elder in the church and always made it to church on Sunday; however, he was not so devoted to me, his oldest son, or others he was responsible for. My father preferred to gamble rather than to feed his family.

Despite everything, I still helped support and loved my family. My mother continued to blame me for her ailments. She had repeatedly burdened me with the guilt that giving birth to me tore her up inside. She blamed me for all her health problems and pains. Throughout her life, she reminded me that I had caused her a lot of pain. I always felt guilty. No matter how much I helped, no matter how much I did, my mother never forgave me. I finally accepted the fact that I could do nothing to make things better for her.

During one visit with my family, my mother had a surprise announcement. "Leon, Jim has taken a job in Houston," she said. "He and your sister are moving to Pasadena, and in fact, they have rented an apartment there. Your father has made some inquiries and it looks like he is going to take a job in Houston also. We are in the planning stages to make the move soon."

Although my older sister and I got along well, I was usually off doing my own thing, so my sister and I didn't share too much of our personal lives. I hadn't known that her husband, Jim, had gotten a job in Houston. "What day you figure you are going to head out?" I asked Mom, the new information spinning through my head.

"As soon as your father finds out about the job he applied for in the Houston area."

"When are you expecting an answer?" I asked.

"How should I know? Ask your dad," my mother snapped.

"Dad," I said, looking at my mother, "do you know when?"

"I should know in the next couple of days," he responded.

Wow. In the oil fields in Texas, I had experienced more wealth than I had ever known before. This was exciting.

"I want to go with y'all," I said. It might have seemed odd that I wanted to be with them, and it's true that I had thought about running away from home many times during my teenage years, but I had been dedicated to my family and had never left, except for the few hours I was gone when I was a senior in high school.

I began telling friends I would be moving to Houston, Texas. I had left some really good friends in Spearman a few months before, and I was just now getting into the swing of hanging out with my new friends. This was a sad time for me, but I was hopeful that this move would lead to success. I felt my life had been improving since I had been to Texas. I had not been going to bed hungry, and I was getting bigger and stronger. I was still able to sleep without the bloody nightmares. I felt ready for the adventure.

I asked a Mormon friend, Gilbert, if he wanted to come along. I had known Gilbert, a friend from Joplin, since we had been four years old. We had gone to church and high school together. At one point, I had loaned Gilbert my Honda 305 Scrambler. Damon later told me that Gilbert had been revving up the engine until it sounded like he was trying to blow the motor. I had approached Gilbert about this, and Gilbert had said he didn't think it would hurt the bike. I just let it go but never let Gilbert use my bike again. Gilbert's stepfather was a Cherokee Indian and a police officer who was not allowed to interact with the public because of his extreme anger issues. Once, when Gilbert was eleven, his dad punched him in the stomach. Asking Gilbert if he wanted to move to Houston was my way of helping a friend, as I knew Gilbert had suffered a lot of abuse at home like I had. This would provide an escape for Gilbert, who was a pocket protector-wearing geek. He responded, "Hell, yeah, I want to come."

My younger sister had become engaged at sixteen years old. She and her fiancé were also coming along. And, of course, my little

66

brother would be making the move. Now we had the entire family, plus two, who were relocating to Pasadena, or as some would call it, Stink-er-dener because of the Shell Oil refinery, the Goodyear plant, and other refineries in that area that emitted a strong odor. The area along the Houston Ship Channel most certainly had its own unique odors and stench from all the chemicals processed there. Houston was hundreds of miles from the Texas Panhandle oil fields where I had worked earlier that year.

"Gilbert, I'll ride with you for a while, then alternate with John," I said when we were ready to make the drive. I supposed that John, my younger sister's finance, might need relief since he was pulling the U-Haul. I had saved some of the Black Mollies and offered one each to Gilbert and John; each swallowed one. We stopped after a few hours and bought some refreshments. Gilbert got a soft drink with caffeine and said he was feeling a little woozy.

"Leon, would you drive my car for a while, so I can rest? I'm feeling a little sleepy," said Gilbert.

About a half an hour after I took the wheel, I barked an order to Gilbert: "Get your ass back in your seat. Just because this piece of crap is a convertible does not mean you are supposed to stand up in it while we are moving." We had crossed the border, 'The Red River,' and now we were in Texas on Interstate 45 heading south toward Houston. Texans say anybody north of the Red River is a damn Yankee. But all of us in this caravan looked more like hillbillies.

Gilbert stood up again. "Wow, man, do you see the birds up there?" he asked.

"I said get your dumb ass back in the seat or I'll stop, tie you up, and stuff your ass in John's trunk," I warned. Gilbert was not handling the amphetamines and Coca Cola well.

"Spoil sport, I was only trying to catch one of those birds." Gilbert sat down as ordered.

We arrived at the residential address (three-bedroom rental house), in Pasadena just off Red Bluff Road a couple of hours after my family had arrived. We helped unload the U-Haul trailer John had pulled and the U-Haul truck my dad had driven. Gilbert had brought his Red Chevrolet Corvair convertible, and John had driven his Red Ford Fairlane two-door, plus he pulled an open-top U-Haul trailer. I had sold my car and had shared rides with Gilbert and others when I wasn't riding my Harley. We looked like modern-day Beverly Hillbillies, kind of like Jed Clampett, Ellie Mae, and Jethro. The open-top trailer and the back seat of the Corvair were stuffed with bikes, personal possessions, and boxes of miscellaneous items. All we needed to complete the look was someone rocking in a chair on top of the trailer while John drove.

"Leon, we're going to church Sunday; you plan on coming?" my mother asked as she tilted her head back and looked down her nose at me.

"I guess so; I don't have anything else planned," I answered. I had seldom attended church since I returned to Missouri after working in the oil fields.

On Sunday, we arrived at church and parked in the large parking lot. As we walked into the building, we were greeted.

"Good morning. I am Brother Johnson. Welcome to Pasadena Ward II."

"Hello, I am Brother Mecham. Me and my family just moved here and thought we would attend church this morning," said my father.

"Do you have a job, a place to live, anything else I can do to help?" Brother Johnson asked.

"Thanks. I have a job, and we have rented a house in Pasadena. The boys here need to find some work, though," my dad said, referring to Gilbert, John, and me.

"Great, let's find Brother Lawton. I think he has been needing some help." We soon found Brother Lawton and discussed jobs for us boys.

Brother Lawton was very helpful. "We have just expanded our business, and we need all the help we can get. I'll write down our address after Sunday School and give it to y'all. Might as well come in the morning if you are all settled in. The job will be repairing pallets. By the way, we have a church basketball league, too, and if any of you boys are interested, let me know. The weekly games will start in a few weeks, but in the meantime, we have basketball practice on Tuesday night."

This appealed to me. At my last high school, where I spent two and a half years, I led my basketball team to the conference playoffs when I was a junior. I had become the leading rebounder and scorer. I always immersed myself in everything I did and followed my grandfather's teaching to always do my best. I worked hard and played hard. I had become very competitive and had been pretty damn good for a high schooler who had played only three years and who'd spent a lot of that time sitting on the bench because of knee injuries. I was naturally athletic, but the knee injuries kept me from earning any athletic scholarships, and it was the knee injuries that kept me from being drafted. I had had my knees drained after the initial injury, and from time to time, whenever I suffered reinjuries, I had been given opioids for pain. I still carried bone fragments in and around my right kneecap. I was somewhat stubborn and impatient, but I was, nevertheless, resilient. Besides, I liked the competition and teamwork of basketball. I was nineteen now, and my knees had been holding up.

Though I had been reluctant to return to church, I now began to think that maybe these guys weren't so bad. Besides, I had noticed a few young ladies around the church, and a couple of them had caught my attention. I had not been dating much since I had broken it off with my high school sweetheart, Linda, two years before. I loved her dearly, but I knew I was not ready to settle down, get married, and have kids. She was!

I was in the main hall of the church when I laid eyes on this girl. She had long shiny black hair, a curvy body, and a pretty smile. I went up to her and introduced myself.

"Hi, my name is Leon, what's yours?"

"Alisa."

"I heard that there was going to be a pool party next Saturday at the townhouse where Mark lives," I offered. "Are you planning on making it to the party?"

"I'm not sure yet," she answered. Alisa was my age. She had beautiful, long, black hair. Her father worked at Shell Oil Refinery, and the family lived about two miles south of the refinery, where the industrial stench was usually noticeable even when the wind was not blowing. When the north wind picked up, the odor was terrible.

Alisa's mother came from German descent, and her father was of mixed heritage that included a bit of Cherokee, which is where Alisa got her brown eyes and beautiful, dark, black hair. Alisa's mother was nurturing — she was a great cook and was always inviting people to stay for dinner.

I became friends with Alisa's brother, Jerry. He taught me how to surf. We developed a Springtime routine. Jerry would check the surf report every Saturday morning at 4 a.m. and call me. Jerry,

Alisa, a friend or two, and I would head to Galveston beach. Some would hang out on the beach while Jerry and I and sometimes others would attempt to surf. Then, we sit around on the beach, eat food we'd brought, laugh, and enjoy each other's company. Just before a storm the waves would get pretty high, but so did the danger factor. We never pushed our luck when the storms were coming in.

At our new job, we did our best, even though it was a crappy, dirty, physically demanding job.

Brother Lawton was a partner in the pallet company, which employed several Mormon boys and a few other employees. The other partner was not a Mormon but was happy that Brother Lawton had an endless supply of fresh Mormon laborers. We boys who worked there were friends at church and friends at work, and we began running around together after hours and on weekends. Sometimes, girls would come along, and we would travel around in groups with two or three carloads of young men and girls. Alisa had begun tagging along with me. We would go in a group to high-end stores in malls and ooh and ahh at the expensive shoes and clothes. One night, we made it down to Love Street near the ship channel by downtown Houston. Love Street was a gathering place for hippies, Banditos, Hell's Angels, prostitutes, and drug dealers. We were there for two reasons: one, to listen to the bands that played the music of Janis Joplin, the Beatles, Rolling Stones, Jimmy Hendrix, and others; and two, to satisfy our curiosity. We posed an unusual sight for the denizens of Love Street. We didn't drink; we didn't do drugs; we didn't curse. We upheld our Mormon teachings. We kept together as a group, and none of us wandered off alone. We really had no idea what all was going on; we were more curious than anything, especially me. One night around 10 p.m., a few Hell's Angels, sporting their long hair, beards, and flying their colors, came roaring in on their badass, chopped Harleys.

A Mormon boy in our group, Dep, approached me. "Hey, Leon, I understand you have a Chopper," he said.

"Yes, I do, it's a '49 Pan."

"I sure would like to see it."

"Come on over tomorrow after church, and I will get it out of the garage," I offered.

"Sure will."

"Do you have a bike?" I asked.

"No, but they sure look like fun. How do you like your bike?"

"I love it. I love working on it and riding it with the wind blowing my face and hair," I said.

It was by chance that our family had moved into the same subdivision where Dep and his family lived. They had a large family, and the two older boys were about the ages of Gilbert, John, and me. It was not unusual to see the five of us together. I had begun to soften up. I had a regular job and now a regular girlfriend. I and my new friends, although they were Mormons, were getting along quite well.

Dep had told me that he had been confused about baptism, as the Mormons and other religions promoted the same idea. The idea was that to get to heaven, one had to be baptized in his or her religion. Dep took that seriously and went to numerous other churches, asking each of them to baptize him, so he had been baptized many times in various religions. Dep eventually told me that his mother was an alcoholic, which was by Mormon standards a serious sin and grounds for excommunication. I understood the levity of his opening up to me.

I had begun to migrate toward Mormonism again. I stopped drinking and fighting. It had been weeks since I had drunk a beer and even a lot longer since I had kicked anybody's ass. I had been thinking about selling my bike and getting a car. I saw an ad that made my eyes light up. I immediately called the number: "Hello, do you have a '55 Nomad for sale?" I asked.

"Sho' do."

"Man, I sure like that model of car; would you be willing to trade your car for a Harley?" I offered.

"Bring it over, and I'll look at your bike. I am at Mo's garage on Scott Street, ten blocks west of Interstate 45." I had no idea about the neighborhood I was heading into. This neighborhood served as headquarters for the national organization of the Black Panthers, and it was known as a place where white people disappeared, and police did not go.

I parked in front of Mo's garage, realizing I was in dark territory. I was a country boy and had never seen a black neighborhood. There were burglar bars on every house, business building, and every building one could put burglar bars on, and there were more black people than I had seen in my entire life. Everyone was looking at me. What, had they never seen a Harley chopper before?

Riding a chopper around Houston, especially on Interstate 45 and most especially riding down Scott Street, was kind of like working on the rig in that something or someone might cause you to die at any second. There were people sitting on their porches, in yards, and walking on the sidewalks. They were all staring at me. A white boy on a motorcycle was a rare sight in this area, and the residents were curious. Nevertheless, I was, as usual, singular in thought and did not allow any emotion to show.

"Afternoon. Are you Mo?" I asked.

"Yea."

"I came to look at your Nomad. This is the bike we told you about."

"It looks like your bike needs a lot of work," Mo said, leading me into the garage and over to the Nomad.

I opened the hood and looked at the engine. I then slowly walked around the Nomad, looking for damage.

"Your car needs a little work, too."

"So, are you interested?" Mo asked.

"I'm gonna pass," I said. I got onto my bike and high-tailed it out of there, having an overwhelming feeling I was not wanted.

• • •

Basketball practice at church evolved into competitive games. The church league was about to start, and I was ready. I had found peace for the time being and was happy living with my family again, working, and going to church regularly. I could not afford my own place, so Gilbert and I had moved in with my parents. Church was, for the most part, a social group I enjoyed being with. Again, there were no confrontations and no fights. One night at practice someone rolled a basketball toward some of us who were shooting baskets. I had gone up for a rebound, and as I came down, the ball rolled under my right foot. My right foot came into contact with the ball, and with my weight on it, I felt a sudden sharp pain in my ankle. I fell to the floor, as my ankle would not support my weight. My friends took me to the hospital. I had fractured my right ankle, and the doctor applied a plaster cast to my lower leg and ankle. I was in bed for a few days, but with the help of crutches, I had some mobility. My ankle had swollen about three times its normal size before I finally gave in to resting it and keeping it elevated. In the meantime, my father's employer had given Dad a self-service gas station to manage. My dad also delivered gas to his employer's other stations. My family found another place to live that was closer to Dad's work. Our new home was a few miles away in La Porte. I had decided to sell my bike, so I put it out front and hung a for-sale sign on it. I sold it within a few days. I had even traded my Bates leather motorcycle jacket for a more conservative winter coat. I had decided it was time to repent for my sinful ways and buckle down. I sold my Harley and used the money to purchase a Ford Falcon, and I wanted to go to college.

• • •

"I would like to enroll for the fall semester, if possible." I was at the registrar's office at San Jacinto Junior College.

The clerk instructed me to fill out some forms and bring them my college transcripts. I had gone to college when I graduated from high school at age 17, but I had taken some really bad advice and ended up failing a five-credit hour algebra and trigonometry course. I had gotten discouraged with higher education. My father had been telling me I was wasting my time. Education was for idiots, he said. But I wanted to try. I enrolled and made it through the first semester, passing all my courses.

It was 1969, and the draft lottery was coming up. I had initially been classified 4-F, due to my bad knees, which were ruined by my high school coach, but I had now been called up by the Army for another physical to check to see if my knees had improved. I reported to the veterans' hospital and met with a military doctor to examine my knees. My knees had not improved, and the Army physician ver-ified that. A few days later, when the lottery was in progress, Gilbert, John, and I sat around the TV waiting for the news. John had mar-ried my little sister only a few days before.

President Nixon stood at the podium in front of the news media for the announcement: "The number one date drawn was September 14." John, Gilbert, and I gasped. Gilbert's birthday was

September 14. Gilbert went directly down to the draft board the next day and volunteered for the draft. Volunteering gave him a little better position than those who did not; nevertheless, he was headed for Vietnam. John went down to the Marine Corps recruiting center and enlisted with the Marines. He was sent to Okinawa. I continued to date Alisa and was getting a strong message from my parents that they wanted me out of the house. My parents kept dropping hints that I was ready to live the Mormon dream of church and family. My mother liked Alisa, and I got along well with her mother and family. They were good Mormons. I wanted out of my parents' house probably as much as they wanted me out. I had been slow in getting my life sorted out, and I still felt like a mixed-up kid. Alisa had graduated from high school and didn't have any plans to go to college. Under Mormon rule, it was time for her to start producing a new generation of Mormons. Although I was unsure, I felt it was time I followed the example others had laid out.

"Alisa, you want to get married?" I popped the question.

"Let me think about it," she said.

A week later, she told me, "If we get married, I want to get married in the Mormon Temple in Mesa, Arizona."

"Wow, I don't know how we are going to do it financially, but we'll find a way," I said.

We made wedding plans. I traded up to a red '67 Mustang, and we made the trip to Mesa with Alisa's parents in tow.

I had progressed through the offices of the church as a good Mormon boy does. I was now ordained as an Elder and had gained status in the church as a man. I had also been tithing and had received a temple recommend, which I needed to get married in the temple. I had gotten so involved in church, I had been appointed to different responsible offices in the ward. I learned that the bishop and his assistants had prayed and had chosen me to become a group leader of the Elders Quorum. I had also accepted assignments in other positions, including that of home teacher. I became recognized as somewhat of a holy man. I performed the "laying on of hands" for the sick, applying virgin olive oil as the Mormons taught me to do. I felt loved and accepted, and beyond that, I began getting more requests to anoint people, to lay my hands on their heads, and pray. Some claimed a miracle had happened after I did this. They claimed they had been instantly healed. On one occasion in particular, the bishop called me.

"Leon, Sister Johns went to the doctor yesterday and was told her white blood count was way off and that they need to do more testing. Would you be able to find a partner and visit her tonight and lay your hands on her?"

"Sure, Bishop James, I will make a couple of calls and get it set up." I never refused to help people, and if this might help her, I was all for it. My assistant and I laid our hands on Sister Johns and said a prayer. She got up, claiming she could feel the spirit and knew she was healed. The next day she went back to her doctor. The medical staff drew some more blood and ran it through the lab. Her blood count showed completely normal. This spooked me a little. The next Sunday, the bishop's first counselor hinted that maybe I should be the next bishop. One didn't become a bishop until he was forty to sixty years old. I was only twenty-one. Me? A bishop?

As usual, I followed my grandfather's teaching to always give it my best and to do everything possible to do things right. I was totally immersed into the Mormon church and was doing everything I could to honor my father and mother.

People seemed to notice. Brother Bill, a well-respected Mormon, met with me and offered me a job with Beneficial Life Insurance Company.

I accepted the job with Beneficial Life, which was owned by the Mormons. The boss was the manager of an agency for the life insurance company, and he was a Mormon. I began selling life insurance for one company and selling health insurance for another. Neither gig was paying much, and now being married, I needed to make more money. By now Alisa was pregnant and was to soon deliver.

"Leon, the company wants you to move to Dallas. I have an office there/You can come into the office every day, and I can help you learn the insurance business. As a result, you'll sell more and bigger policies with bigger commissions," Brother Elston, another associate, said.

I was excited about this new offer and rushed home to discuss it with Alisa.

I told her what Brother Elston had said. "He has a position in Dallas and an office I can work out of. He assured me that I'll be making more money. He suggested that I drive up on Monday morning and look around. I told him I would come up and look. He and his wife are going to let me stay at their house for a few days, so it won't cost much to go up there and stay the week. I'll also get some 'one-on-one' training that I believe will help."

"Okay, I'll stay here and keep my job for the time being," Alisa said. She did not like the idea of moving away from her mother, but she agreed to move after I established myself in the new job.

Dallas was somewhat smaller and was much easier to get around in than Houston was. I quickly got comfortable with the town and the work, as Brother Elston began teaching me a few things. I made a couple of sales that week and headed back to Pasadena. I was there when my first son was born. The first time I held my son, I got choked up, and tears came to my eyes. I had a son. I vowed to treat my son better than my father had treated me. I continued to travel to Dallas on Mondays and back on Fridays. Alisa got stronger, and I found a place in Grand Prairie where we could live. It was old military housing from WWII. The area was poor, but the people in the neighborhood were good people. So, I moved my small family to the Dallas area.

Shortly after the move to Grand Prairie, things started to erode with Brother Elston and Beneficial Life Insurance Company. A couple of the policies I sold had been canceled, and I was not doing as well as I or Brother Elston had hoped I would. I hated going into the office every day. I had always been an outdoors person and had never felt totally comfortable selling insurance.

My grandfather Hank had been a carpenter and had taught me a little bit about the trade. I knew I needed to find a job that would support my family. I decided to look around for outdoor work.

I found a housing subdivision under construction and drove up to the site. There was a small group of men standing near the street, so I stopped and called to the person who appeared to be in charge. "Y'all doing any hiring?"

Bill, the foreman, looked at me. "Yes, how soon can you start? Do you have any experience? Do you have any tools?"

"No, but I can start tomorrow."

"Be here at 7 a.m. sharp; you can pick up a tool here and there as you go."

I showed up the following morning and began my new career as a carpenter's helper. I put my heart and soul into it. I was ecstatic to be working outside again at a job I enjoyed. Now I was following the trade my grandfather had worked in. This could be what I was meant to do. None of my other jobs gave me the satisfaction that carpentry did. It did not pay much, but I put everything into my job anyway. After a few months, I was talking to Jody, a carpenter on my crew, about my position and pay.

Jody told me, "Dicky and I are going to start our own framing crew. I have been watching your work, and we are interested in you being our helper. We are only going to be a crew of three, so it will give you an opportunity to learn a lot more, and your education will be a lot faster than working on this large crew. On top of that, we will pay you 25% percent more per hour. We will also let you do a little subcontracting on some of the smaller tasks if you like." I agreed to go to work for them.

My six-foot, four-inch frame towered over both Jody and Dicky, who were each about five-feet-nine, tops. They nicknamed me Big K. The K was for Kryptonite, which was the only thing that could defeat Superman. They joked with me about being stronger than Superman. It was good humor most of the time, but sometimes their joking around was sort of like picking on me. I was good natured, though, and endured their friendly jokes and pranks.

One afternoon Jody met up with me.

He said, "Hey, Leon, it's Friday and we always go get some beer at lunch and ice it down for after work. Would you like to come?"

"Sure, let's go," I agreed. I was once again taken in by the crew and taught the routine. I had started drinking again and wanted to hang with the boys. I felt good about following in my grandfather's footsteps working as a carpenter. With this job, I was not only work-ing but also learning a skilled trade, and I took great pride in that. No more laborer, I wanted to be a carpenter. Not only had my grand-father been a carpenter, but Christ himself had been one also, and I was trying to be as good a Mormon as I could be, except now I was enjoying beer. The crew I was on was framing high-end houses. Residential construction was going crazy, and there was not enough labor to keep up with the demands in the Dallas/Fort Worth area. With the economy and labor as they were, houses could not be built fast enough.

I had been working for Dicky and Jody for a short time as a carpenter's helper, and I had been throwing newspapers on the weekend for a little more income. I had to get up at 3 a.m. on Saturday morning and 2 a.m. on Sunday morning. I worked about forty hours a week doing carpentry, played softball in the afternoons and evenings, and played for two different teams in two leagues, one church league and the other a city league. Then on weekends I threw or placed the newspapers on a commercial route in downtown Dallas. Then I attended church on Sundays, attended at least two, mostly three meetings, and one meeting on Wednesday. I was busy, tired, and numb. I was still a mixed-up kid and was only going through the motions of what I thought I should be doing — maybe more importantly, following my parents' teachings, my grandfather's teachings, and the teachings of the Mormons. There were numerous conflicts with the things I had been taught. I had seen my father steal and had seen both parents take drugs while they were telling me to follow the Ten Commandments. Mormons preached love and forgiveness, yet my mother never forgave me for hurting her during my birth. She reminded me of this every chance she got. I worked and played to the point of exhaustion, so I could sleep a little. I had not slept well for years. The message was work, honest and hard, attend church, get married, and have children. These were some of the teachings I had followed through on and was now living, but I was still unsettled. I thought I just needed to keep on doing what I was doing as I had hopes that I was headed in the right direction, but I was not feeling it. I still did not feel at peace.

One day, Jody said to me, "If you want to, you can install the gyprock on this house after hours." Gyprock is mostly used for moisture barrier and sheathing and is installed on the outside of the exterior walls. "We'll pay you $40 extra, but if you take the job, you have to have it finished in three evenings." It was between seasons for sports, so I jumped on the chance to make a little more money so I could better provide for my wife and son.

I learned to measure, cut, and install gyprock. It was the same process as installing drywall. I finished the gyprock job and completed the subcontract job within the time limit agreed on. I got paid for it on Friday along with my hourly pay. Jody and Dicky agreed to let me have all the gyprock jobs on the houses they were framing. They also informed me that they were going to work more Saturdays as fall was coming and there would be some rain days and freezing days coming up in the winter that would not allow us to work outside. I agreed that working Saturdays would be good. I was beginning to feel more like a carpenter and was learning more every day. My confidence in my ability to learn also increased. My parents had focused on being Mormons and on making their children Mormons. I was now beginning to grow beyond their teachings. I was becoming myself, slowly but surely.

Bruce Lee said, "The most important thing in life is for every individual to get to know themselves." I still had a long way to go!

The Panhead, my first Harley.

Me (in the middle), my friends, and our bikes.

Easy ridin' during my biking days.

CHAPTER 3

Construction, Carpentry, and Separation

I had settled in with the new people in the Mormon church in Dallas, and I'd found a rhythm with team sports. I had made it through the winter, and now spring had arrived; softball season was about to start. I was accepted on the softball team and alternated between playing center and right field. I wasn't speedy, so I relied on anticipation and was able to get the jump on many a play. As the season went on, I got comfortable and became a good hitter, usually reaching base.

One afternoon, we were playing another Mormon team from the area. I had been asked to play first base since the usual first baseman was a no show. The visitors' dugout was close to first base. The first baseman for the other team had been heckling me and others in the initial innings. The heckler was now up to bat. He hit a ball over my head, and it dropped into shallow right field for a base hit. Royce, a teammate, picked up the ball and quickly fired it to second base just as the runner had rounded first base and was headed for second. In anticipation of a play on the base runner, I fell in behind the runner and was following him to second base. As the runner was making his way to second, Bill, the cutoff man, caught the ball and readied himself for a throw to me. The base runner turned and realized I was between him and first base. He began to run back to first as I caught the ball in my glove and met the runner coming toward me. I had covered the ball in my glove with my right hand so it wouldn't pop out and I wouldn't drop it. As the runner and I met in the baseline, I reached out with both arms and tagged the runner in the mouth with my glove, tagging him out and rendering him nearly unconscious.

"I've had enough of your mouth," I said with a steely stare. No more needed to be said. The other team wilted as the heckler had been keeping their energy going. Now you could see the spirit was drained from the entire team. Even though it was hotter than blue blazes, I, as usual, put all my energy into whatever I was doing. Although this play might have been a little over the top, it stopped the heckling.

When it was my turn to bat, the opposing team's right fielder had set up a little close in, I noticed. When I came up to bat, I dug in the toe of my right foot, tipped the bat over my right shoulder and *crack*, I hit the ball over the right fielder's head and took off running. I easily tagged first and second bases. As I rounded the baseline for third base, I was running as hard and as fast as I could. The third baseman caught the ball just as I was coming down the baseline. In my peripheral vision, I had seen the ball coming and prepared for a slide. The third baseman was a large guy with a more than ample stomach, and I did not see any point in colliding with him, as he outweighed me by at least fifty pounds. I went into a slide leading with my right foot, ankle high and left foot slightly raised. My steel-cleated shoe made contact with the third baseman's ankle and took the fielder's feet out from under him. The third baseman turned his body and began to fall toward me. Seeing that the third baseman was about to fall on me, I lifted my left foot and vaulted the big guy up and over. I half rolled, half crawled the short distance to third base. "*Safe!*" called the third base umpire. I had always been competitive, and when I felt it was warranted, I would ramp up the intensity of my play.

Back in the dugout, Royce sat next to me. "Dang, Leon, I think you hurt that big guy."

"I had enough heckling from the first baseman, and the third baseman was blocking my path. It was the only play I could think of to get to third base without getting hurt. I wasn't about to stand there and let him fall on me or tag me out if I could help it," I said.

I gained a widespread reputation for intense play. For me, it was about playing hard by giving my best, competing fairly, and winning. My philosophy was, "Why compete if you don't plan to win?" My grandfather never discussed losing, and I rarely ever lost at anything I tried.

In my life in general, I had been feeling pressure and felt that something had to give. I had my family, my carpentry work, church meetings, Mormon work, home teaching, and weekend newspaper deliveries. I needed to adjust my schedule. I let Brother Baker know I'd be dropping the paper route. He was understanding.

Jody had decided to sell his '64 Ford pickup, and I bought it. I now had my first pickup and had accumulated a few tools, many of which I got from pawn shops. Using some scrap wood, I built a wooden toolbox and installed it in the bed of my pickup. I was beginning to feel like a skilled laborer. With my focus and skills, I could produce more work in any given day than most of my co-workers could.

At church, I ran into the bishop. Bishop Richardson asked me to meet with him after Sunday School. He did not give me any idea as to why.

With some trepidation, I made it to the bishop's office, tapped lightly on the door, and went in.

"Yes, Bishop, you wanted to see me. What can I do for you?"

"Leon, it has come to the attention of the Bishopric that you could be more involved with the members. You have been doing a great job as an Elder and after praying about it, we would like you to accept the office of 'Seventy.' As a Seventy, you'll have different responsibilities from what you now have. The families you now visit will be reassigned to another Elder, and we want you to work primarily with the missionaries. The families you will be assigned to are either new members, non-active members, or members who rarely come to meetings."

It was a great privilege and honor to be called to such an office in the Mormon church, but it was a double-edged sword. I was beside myself with pride that I had been offered such a very responsible position, and I quickly accepted. I was hoping it would change only what I was doing for the church and not add to the number of hours it took to do the work. There were only twenty-four hours in a day, and I did need to sleep.

The Bishopric, consisting of the bishop and his two counselors, met with me, laid their hands on my head, and prayed. They appointed me to my new office later that evening. I entered my new responsibility with a "get -'er -done" attitude.

I told my family of my new appointment.

"Congratulations, Leon. That is really an honor!" my older sister said, excited for me.

"That is an important position, Leon. Do you think you are ready for it?" my dad asked.

"Yes, Dad. The Bishopric would not have offered it to me if they did not think I could handle it."

My mother said, scowling, "Time will tell."

I felt deflated and doubted whether I had made the right decision. I wanted to believe I had. The Bishopric had prayed on it and asked whether I was confident that I would do the very best I could.

I traveled with the missionaries by car sometimes, but mostly we rode bicycles. The missionaries and I met with the families I had been assigned to. On one visit, I went alone, unannounced, to see a family I had been unable to reach by phone. They had been missing church.

I approached the modest, one-story home and knocked on the door. "Good evening. Is Brother John home?" The young brunette who answered the door held an infant on her hip.

"No, he had an accident and is in the hospital," she said.

I gently asked what had happened, and she explained that John had been working on his hot rod when the engine backfired.

"He had his greasy coveralls on, and they caught on fire. He got burned really bad before we could get the fire out and his coveralls off. It was terrible," she sobbed. "We called 911, and the ambulance came."

She explained that John had been taken to Parkland Hospital, where he was in the burn unit.

"How's he doing?" I asked.

"He's going to make it, but we've been told he will need several skin grafts and surgeries. I just don't know what I am going to do with the new baby and all."

89

I patted her shoulder and looked into her eyes. "If you need anyone to listen, please call us. We are here to help you through this," I said, adding that my partner and I would visit John if she thought he'd like us to.

"I think that would be great," she said. "Thank you." She was grateful to have the attention and concern of a Seventy.

I called my teaching partner, Steve, and explained the situation. The next day, we drove to Parkland Hospital, the same hospital where President Kennedy was taken in 1963 when he was shot.

As we entered the hospital, we stopped at the front desk, and I gave the receptionist a smile. "Hi, we're here to see Brother John; I understand he's in the burn ward."

She instructed us to go to the nurses' station for the burn unit on the fourth floor. We found the elevator, rode it up, and exited into a sterile white hallway with a busy nurses' station directly in front of us. We approached and waited until the nurse sitting behind the desk asked if she could help us.

"We have come to see Brother John. We understand he is in this unit."

"Do you have permission to go into the burn ward? There are restrictions," the dour-looking nurse challenged.

I pulled from my wallet a card to be used in this kind of situation. I had learned that when I became a Seventy, I was qualified to apply for a ministerial license. Apparently, the Bishopric of the Mormon church had submitted the paperwork, received the ministerial license in my name, and had given me the card shortly after I had accepted the position of Seventy. This was the first time I had any reason to show the card to anyone. I was a licensed, card-carrying minister ready to help any way I could.

"Excuse me, Doctor," said the nurse to an arriving physician. "This is Leon; he is a licensed minister and wishes to go into the burn ward and visit one of the patients."

The doctor took a closer look at me, clearly surprised to see that someone so young was an ordained minister.

"Well, come with me then," said the doctor, and he led Steve and me to a station just outside the burn ward, where we got masks, gowns, and footies to put over our shoes. The doctor explained it was extremely important to keep the burn ward free of germs, as the patients were highly susceptible to infections. The additional articles of clothing we would wear would reduce the possibility of bacteria getting to the patients. Severe burns ravage the skin down to the fat, and some of the fat also gets burned, leaving the patient with a lot less insulation to keep their bodies warm. Most of the patients in this ward were not wearing clothes, which exposed them to any bacteria in the room, and they had heat lamps around them to help keep their body temperature within the normal range.

The doctor pointed down the hallway to a set of double doors. "That is the way to the burn ward. There should be a nurse available to direct you to John's bed."

I thanked the doctor as Steve and I headed in the direction of the burn ward. I was not looking forward to seeing Brother John's condition but knew that he would need spiritual healing to help him through the trying times that lay ahead.

As we entered the ward, we saw a nurse and asked where we might find Brother John.

"He's in the second row, five beds back on the left. Are you a relative?" she asked.

"No," I responded as I pulled my ministerial card from my wallet. "I am an ordained minister who came to visit and provide spiritual support to Brother John."

I had to swallow when I saw John. He was lying on his bed with the front of his body exposed. He had severe burns on his upper arms, chest, and stomach. The damaged skin ranged from red and swollen to no longer there. I looked into John's eyes.

"Good evening, Brother John, how are you feeling?"

"Not so good. And they say it's only going to get worse," he replied, sounding heavily medicated.

"How the heck did this happen?" I asked.

Brother John paused, then said, "Oh, you know my old hot rod?"

"Yes, it's bright yellow, isn't it?" I said.

"Canary yellow." He slowly continued, "I had changed out the intake manifold and had put a new Edelbrock aluminum high-rise intake on it. I had also put in a new 850 cfm Holley four- barrel carburetor."

"Nice."

"I was getting the distributor in time and the carburetor adjusted when I asked my wife to turn over the engine. She tried turning the engine over a few times while I made final adjustments to the distributor. As you know, the distributor is at the back of the motor, and as I was reaching over the carburetor, the engine backfired. My greasy overalls caught on fire! I started screaming and running. Slapping at the flames. Somehow, I remembered the instructions from the TV commercial, so I stopped, dropped, and rolled around on the ground. My wife jumped out of the car, grabbed the fire extinguisher, chased me down, and sprayed me. I was already badly burned in the couple of minutes it took."

"You were lucky she reacted like she did," I noted.

"My wife saved my life!" he said.

I asked him if he needed anything, and he asked, "Since you're here, would you mind laying your hands on my head and saying a prayer for me? I'm really in severe pain, and not even the morphine is helping much."

We anointed Brother John's head with oil and laid our hands on his head. The room grew quiet, and it seemed as though the air between Brother John and me grew lighter, feeling sort of electrified. As I spoke, Brother John's face relaxed. It was an extremely moving experience.

As I finished my prayer and was saying good-bye to Brother John, the patient in the next bed slightly waved his hand, catching my attention.

"Do you need something?" I asked. This patient had severe burns on the left side of his face and body down to his knees. I moved closer.

"Would … you … mind saying… a… prayer for me?" he softly whispered.

"I would be happy to," I said, signaling for Steve to join me.

Other patients, upon witnessing what was going on, had felt the same energy and asked for the same attention. Before we left the room, every burn patient in the ward had requested we perform the laying on of hands. I was elated; I liked helping others. If a little olive oil and laying on of hands helped someone feel better, then I was on board. I could be as gentle and soft as a newborn pup or as rough as oil field trash.

I wasn't always as attuned to my own health needs, though. I had a history of environmental allergies, and that year the pollen and dust seemed to be worse than ever. I came down with a sinus infection in the fall. Remembering Red's advice from back in my oil days, I thought, "I can feel bad at home, or I can go to work, still feel bad, and get paid."

I managed to work and perform my church duties. But one morning, I felt too bad to go to work. I called in to say that I was running a fever, felt weak, and would be seeing a doctor.

Alisa drove me to the small hospital where my doctor maintained his office. She dropped me at the door and went to park. I entered through the double sliding doors and walked up to the check-in counter.

"Nurse, I am feeling really tired. Is there someplace I can lie down?" I asked.

She pointed to a gurney in the nearby hallway and asked if I thought I could make it there.

"I'm not sure. Can you help me?" I was feeling very weak.

The nurse, concerned that I might fall, came around the desk and put her arm around my back at my waist. I was dizzy and weak and appreciated her help. As she helped me lie down, I felt myself collapsing as I passed out.

Alisa, entering the emergency room, saw me as I passed out on the gurney, and she rushed over.

"What's wrong? What happened?" Her fear was tangible.

"We don't know at this time. A doctor will examine him shortly," explained the nurse, and she asked Alisa for my information.

A short time later, in an examination room, the doctor examined me and touched me to get my attention. He asked, "Can you hear me, Leon?"

I struggled to open my eyes. I could not focus, but I could hear someone speaking.

"We're admitting you to the hospital; we think that you have double pneumonia. In any event, your temperature is 103 degrees, and you need to stay here for a day or two."

I passed out again; I was so weak I didn't care what the doctor was saying.

Once I got settled into a room, Alisa left to go take care of the boys and said she would check on me later.

My doctor informed me that I had some scar tissue in my lungs, probably from the childhood pneumonia I had suffered. I spent one of the most boring weeks of my life in the hospital. I was not used to the sedentary life and wanted to get out. When I was discharged, I spent a couple of days at home recovering and regaining my strength. Once I had left the hospital and had to do things for myself, I realized how weak I was. I'd get exhausted and breathless just walking from the bedroom to the bathroom. Although I wanted to get back to work, I enjoyed the extra time I was spending with my boys.

When I finally returned to work, my friends said they had missed me and were glad I was back. I had been doing well at work and had learned a lot. The work was very satisfying, and I was proud to be a carpenter. After having worked at dairy farming and in the oil fields, I found construction to be less physically demanding. I worked only eight hours a day and never more than six days a week. With electric power tools, we could not work in the rain, so there were also rainy days to break the routine.

Fall came upon us quickly; flag football leagues were starting up, and teams were being formed to play in the city league. I was invited to join a team in a city-wide league. A couple of other Mormon boys were also invited to join the team. The players' pools were made up of mostly ex-high school football players and a few guys who had played for a college team here and there.

The season progressed, and the playoffs were coming up. Our team had won a couple of games in the tournament and had moved forward into the finals.

Just before a game was set to start, the coach found me. He asked me to fill in on defensive tackle, as the regular player would be out.

"Okay, no problem, Coach," I agreed.

We were in the third quarter, and we were behind, 7-0. We had just punted the football after failing to score again.

The center on the other team hiked the ball to the quarterback. I had anticipated the snap count, and within a split second, I had broken through the line and was rushing the quarterback. The quarterback realized that I had gotten the jump on the offensive lineman and was going to get his flag and down the ball. The quarterback stopped, set his feet, and fired the cold, hard, leather football, hitting me in the center of my face. I had left my feet to block the pass, thinking the quarterback was trying to throw over my outstretched arms. I was in the air when the football made contact. I blacked out as I fell to the ground, jamming both of my knees. The ref did not call a foul, although one would have been justified, and it would have been a controversial call.

I was helped off the field, and someone brought me a couple of ice packs.

"Leon, how bad is it? Can you still play?" asked Coach.

"I don't know."

"Without you, we will only have ten players, not the required eleven, and will have to forfeit the game."

"Help me stand up," I said.

The coach and my best friend helped me to my feet, but I put weight on my knees, I felt pain shoot up and down my legs. I wasn't certain my knees would support me.

"Give me a minute, and I'll do what I can," I said.

My knees were hurting and throbbing, and I could barely stand up, but I thought of myself as pretty tough and didn't want to let my team down.

"If you can just stand on the field in the middle of the defense, that will give us eleven players, and we can continue to play," Coach said.

I got my bruised knees and legs moving and was able to clear my head a little. I walked onto the field. As I got into position, I considered what the other team's options were and what they were likely to do. I set up, and the center hiked the ball to the quarterback, who, with malicious intent, looked directly at me. Out of the corner of my eye, I saw the left end come down the field and cut right. I knew something was up. First, the opposing quarterback had intentionally injured me by throwing the football directly into my face, which caused me to injure my knees. Now they planned to take advantage of my injured knees. This poor sportsmanship infuriated me, especially since I was the intended target. The receiver's route put his path directly in front of me and only a couple of steps away. They knew that I could not move fast enough to intercept or block the ball and would be slow in getting out of the way. I was an easy mark. I figured it was payback time. I took a couple of steps toward the receiver as he caught the ball, and I delivered my left elbow into the middle of the receiver's face. His feet flew out from under him as his head and upper body went backward. He landed flat on his back, all the air knocked out of him. The receiver was flopping on the ground, sucking air, trying to fill his lungs.

"Screw you, asshole," I said, leaning over the receiver. Now the fight was on. Members of the other team streamed onto the field, trying to get to me. My team came quickly to my defense. The field broke out into one, large chaotic fight.

The referees broke up the fight and ejected me, causing our team to forfeit. We hadn't had a chance of winning the game after I had been injured. The opposing team had eleven healthy players, so no shame in losing, as far as I was concerned. I figured we might as well get the game over with, go home, and nurse our injuries. I turned to walk off the field and almost collapsed because of my knees. A couple of friends helped me off the field and to my pickup.

Fall quickly turned to winter, and an early hard freeze hit Texas in late October. The winter was going to be a bad one. Many days that winter the crew and I were not able to work because of freezing rain and a few snowstorms. In January a freezing rain iced everything over. We worked every day and on weekends when we could. We built fires in 55-gallon barrels and warmed our hands and feet as needed. Some days very little got done because of the colder-than-usual days. We sometimes had to chip ice off the top plates on top of the wall so they could lay out the joists or trusses and install them. But I would do whatever it took to provide for my family.

Finally, spring was coming. It had been the worst winter in a long time. I had been buying a tool here and there, building up my inventory. Jody had even spent a little extra time with me to teach me how to cut rafters, hips, and valleys.

With the arrival of spring, I had a new opportunity. I had heard that Martin, who organized and managed a number of framing crews, needed more framing crews. I knew a couple of guys who were looking for work. I quit working for Jody and Dicky and began framing tract homes as a contractor with my own crew. I got paid based on the square footage of the living area and the square footage of the garage and porches. If anything was left over after wages and expenses, then I got paid. Usually, it was a lot better than what I had been getting paid as a skilled laborer. I could read blueprints, lay out walls, ceiling joists, and cut rafters.

Meanwhile, my old Ford pickup was leaking a lot of oil and was having a few other maintenance issues common for high-mileage, older vehicles. I decided to buy a new pickup. I did not feel comfortable getting an expensive Chevy Silverado. I felt a half-ton would not be strong enough for my needs, and I did not need all the options that came with the Silverado, so I purchased a new three-quarter-ton Chevy Custom pickup with the bare necessities. This truck would haul anything I needed and would get me anywhere I needed to go.

I asked a Mormon buddy, a welder, to help me build and install an overhead rack so I could haul long pieces of lumber and sawhorses for scaffolding.

Martin admired my new pickup truck and offered me an opportunity to put it to work. I framed a few houses for Martin; then he approached me with another opportunity.

"Leon, I have some houses coming up in Graham, Texas, for Mr. Buckman. We need a framer pretty quickly. Would you like to frame some houses in Graham?"

"Yes, sir, when do you need me?" I was eager to start this new project and to prove myself.

As soon as I finished up the current assignment, I'd be heading to Graham.

I told Alisa about the work and the travel it would require. "I'll be staying in a hotel. Would you like to come along and bring our son?" I entreated.

I liked being a father and wanted to have my son nearby. Alisa had not worked for a while, and I figured she could use a change of scenery. She seemed to be very moody. She was pregnant again and would be delivering our second child around April.

We made the trip to Graham, and we had framed a couple of houses when Mr. Buckman approached me with a proposition.

"The project is to build a lumber yard, complete with a retail store," he said. "I know you have worked residential, and you are really good at it. Just thought you might like a new challenge."

I tapped my finger against my chin as though I were giving it some thought. In reality, I was jumping with excitement. This would be a new learning opportunity.

He handed me a set of blueprints in a cardboard tube and asked me to review them. After work, back at the hotel, I told Alisa about his new challenging project.

Alisa dully asked, "Where is this new project?"

"It is here in Graham," I said.

"I was hoping we could head back home. I don't like it here," she said. "I don't have any friends, and there are only three channels on TV. And there isn't a yard for our son to play in. I have to entertain him all day. It's tiring."

We started to make plans for the coming weeks. I offered to drive Alisa and our son back home and spend the weekend with them. Then, on Monday, I'd take the crew back to Graham and begin the new project.

It took us about nine weeks to successfully complete the work on the retail commercial building. It had been a huge undertaking for a young and upcoming carpentry contractor, but I never flinched. I knew what needed to be done and how it needed to get done. I faced each challenge as it came up and worked through it. The project went smoothly and was completed before the deadline.

I was not feeling good about leaving Alisa at home, but I felt worse about dragging her around and making her stay in a hotel room all day. Being on the road made her irritable. And the situation wasn't about to get any easier.

After we finished Mr. Buckman's project, I met with Martin, who told me that Mr. Buckman was ready to start his housing addition in Graham. "My cousin is from there and wants to move back there and take care of Mr. Buckman's framing needs," Martin said.

This was a job that had been promised to me.

"Sorry," said Martin, "but like I said, my cousin wants to move back to Graham and do the framing."

"What kind of experience does he have?" I asked.

"Not your concern. He will be doing the job," Martin ended the conversation.

I felt slighted and hurt because I had wanted that job and had done excellent work for Martin. I had been considering moving my family to Graham. I accepted the politics of the situation and left Graham to Martin's cousin. Besides, Martin had all the work I could handle back in the Dallas-Fort Worth Metroplex. On top of that, I had bought a house for my growing family and myself.

Because of all the travel, I hadn't been attending church regularly, but back in the Metroplex, I got back into the routine of going to church with Alisa and our son. Our second son was born. I was getting better and better at carpentry, and I spent as much time as I could with Alisa and our sons. I still worked long hours and quite a few Saturdays and Sundays as time and weather permitted or demanded, but I took my family to church on some Sundays and participated in any and all events I thought I should be a part of or was asked to do.

I still played softball with the church team, and when the coach died from a sudden heart attack, I, at just thirty-four years old, took charge as coach. Everybody was shocked by the coach's passing, and when the team got together, I stepped up and spoke my piece.

"Bill, the team will be a lot better if you're willing to play second base. I think that's a natural position for you. Royce, with your speed and arm strength, you'll help the team more in center field. I will be playing shortstop. Let's try this defensive lineup and see what happens," I said.

We began winning every game and won the local playoffs in the Mormon league. We were to play in the regional playoffs, but to participate, each player had to wear a baseball cap. No one in the Mormon leagues wore baseball caps; no one had ever discussed wearing baseball caps. This change of rules as we were entering the playoffs made no sense. Why change the rules now? This was very upsetting to me. I told the officials that if I had to wear a cap to satisfy some jerk who wanted to make up arbitrary rules, I was not interested in playing. I never played slow pitch softball again with the Mormons. I was more interested in my career, anyway.

I had another year under my belt and had earned a reputation as a high-quality carpenter who was dependable and had integrity. I had been working a lot of weekends now that I had my own crew. I was entirely in charge of my schedule except when the weather was in charge of my schedule. There was more work than there were workers in the labor force in the Metroplex, and I decided it was time to make some money, so I immersed myself in producing as much as I could.

I also wanted to further my education.

I discussed it with Alisa, telling her I'd like to take a couple of evening classes in the upcoming fall semester. I enrolled in two classes, accounting and business management, both freshman, entry-level college courses. As I walked into the classroom to attend my first class in accounting, the professor met me. He told me the class had been overbooked, that there was no room for me, and he suggested I visit the registrar's office to get a different class assignment.

At the registrar's office, I learned that most of the classes I wanted to take were full. Then I saw it: an opening in Psychology 101. Well, why the hell not? I figured if I worked toward a degree, the class could count as an elective. I had heard of Sigmund Freud and was curious about him and psychology. I enrolled in the psychology class and in business management. I had taken a literature course and a couple of other classes right after high school. I had also taken a college course or two when I was about twenty years old. I was older now and more focused; I knew more about what I wanted and didn't want. I decided to major in business management.

I walked into the psychology class. The professor was almost a foot shorter than I and about seven years older. He welcomed me and introduced himself as Professor James. Then he asked if I'd ever played basketball.

"Yes, I played a little in high school," I said, wondering where this conversation was heading.

"I played point guard," Professor James said.

"I played power forward and a little center," I countered.

"Maybe we could shoot some hoops sometime," the professor offered.

I felt an immediate connection with Professor James. This was the beginning of a life-long friendship with the man who would be my favorite teacher of all time. I would see just how much this man cared about doing his job well and about helping others.

After a few weeks of teaching about the history of psychology and of the masters — Pavlov, Freud, Jung, Messmer, Whaley, Malott and others — Professor James told us to put our books, papers, and pens away. He was going to introduce us to what he called self-hypnosis/deep relaxation. He invited us to close our eyes as he led the class through a breathing exercise. Fifteen minutes passed before the exercise ended, but I felt as if I had just closed my eyes. I felt more peaceful than I had felt in a long, long time. I was unaware of it, but this peace was what I had been searching for. Following what I'd learned from my professor, I practiced deep breathing and meditation every night at home. I had found a way to relax and get to sleep. My sleep became more peaceful and restful than it had been in a very long time.

Christmas was nearing, and a friend, Buddy, was having a very difficult time financially. He told me that he had a car for sale and needed only a couple of hundred dollars so he could get his kids a little something for Christmas. I agreed to look at his car for sale. I drove up to his house, and Buddy came out and met me, saying, "The car is in that barn."

As we walked into the barn, I saw a white 1965 Chevrolet Impala Super Sport. There was one eighth-inch hole in the hood where an intake stack had been. When Buddy opened the hood, I saw a Chevy 396 with a three-barrel, 1050 cfm, Holley carburetor. Buddy said that the cylinders had bored sixty over and that the heads had been sent to Mullins, Indiana, where they were fine-tuned to match the Mullins full race cam he had installed. The bumpers, rear seat, hub caps, and front passenger seat had been removed for drag racing. This car had only 20,000 original miles on it, and the parts that had been removed were stacked and preserved in the hay behind the car. With the exception of the hole in the hood, this car was in immaculate condition.

I asked Buddy how much he wanted for the car.

"Give me two hundred dollars. That will take care of the things I need for Christmas," he said.

I wrote my friend a check; this was an absolute steal. The car didn't run, so I had to borrow a trailer to get it and tow it home. Buddy assured me that it would run great but that the battery was dead; otherwise, all it needed was a new starter.

At home, Alisa asked what I intended to do with the car.

"Look, Alisa, I know we don't need this car, but I got it so cheap, I couldn't pass it up," I told her. "I believe I can work on it a little, sell it, and get another car to replace the one we sold to Royce. This can be a profitable purchase; besides, Buddy was really strapped for money, and we had a little extra." We had been growing apart, and this was another point of contention for her.

"It's a stick shift. I can't drive a stick shift, and you know it," she dug in deeper.

"Look, I'll fix it up and sell it as quickly as I can," I promised. I put in a new starter and battery, and just as Buddy had promised, the car started. I found a replacement hood at the junkyard and for a few dollars was able to replace the damaged one. The headers had pinholes in them, so I drove the car to the muffler shop and got the holes fixed. I advertised the car, and a buyer who was driving a '69 El Camino came to look at it.

"It looks and sounds good. Would you be interested in trading for my El Camino?" the buyer asked.

"What kind of trade are you looking for?" I asked.

"My El Camino is four years newer. It has a 327 4 barrel, headers, and has been bored .40 over. It runs on the streets and has plenty of extra horsepower. I think it is worth $500 and your '65 Impala."

I had just put new tires on the Impala. I offered: I'll give you the $500 and the Impala, but I keep the new tires." The new tires would fit on the El Camino. I felt I had traded up in value. The Impala needed too much work and was going to be expensive to maintain. Besides, it was a full-on drag racing car, pushing around 500 horsepower.

"Deal," we agreed and shook hands.

When I pulled into my driveway, Alisa came storming out the door, her face red with anger.

"What the heck is that, Leon?"

"I just traded the Impala plus $500 for this El Camino. It is four years newer than the Impala and is in a lot better condition."

"That is the ugliest vehicle I have ever seen, and you can't drive the four of us around. It only has a front seat."

"We all will fit in the front seat if we need to. Besides, we still have your car, which has a front and back seat."

"How am I supposed to drive that thing?"

"It's automatic, same as your car."

"I don't like it," Alisa said, stomping back into the house.

I had a job, worked a lot of hours, and now I had a project — the El Camino. Alisa didn't care for it, but it was an automatic, so she could drive it if need be, and it didn't need any repairs. I put the Impala's new tires on the El Camino. It could use some fresh paint, but what the hell, I was in it for less than $1,000.

At work one day, we were waiting for a material delivery, so one of my crew and I decided to go shopping. I had developed the habit of searching in pawn shops for saws, hammers, tool belts, and other necessities of the trade. I could always use extra tools for when crew men forgot their tools or didn't have what they needed. I also bought used circular saws because I could replace the brushes, switches, and other small component parts, allowing me to use the saws until I wore them completely out. After we had scoured the pawn shops, we drove around town to check out what was going on in other housing subdivisions under construction. We had lunch and went back to the project, but still no lumber. I told my crew that I'd see them in the morning; maybe the materials would have shown up by then.

I drove home. As I turned the corner onto our street, I encountered a sight that froze me with fear. About five doors down from my house, I saw my two sons by themselves. My three-year-old was sitting on the curb with his feet in the street, and my one-year-old was in his diaper and sitting on the sidewalk. I was beside myself. My sons could step into the street in front of a moving car and be killed. My heart pounded audibly as I drove to where my sons were. Not wanting to frighten the boys, I came to a controlled stop, got out, put my boys into my truck, and proceeded to our house. I was worried. Has something happened to Alisa? Why were the boys out wandering the street by themselves?

"What in the hell is going on? Where the hell is Alisa?" I spoke out loud as I hammered my palm against the steering wheel.

At home, I gathered the boys, led my three-year-old and carried my one-year-old up the steps to the front door. As I opened the door, I could hear the television broadcasting a soap opera. I looked toward the couch and saw Alisa lying there, asleep, still in the same clothes she had slept in the night before. I began to seethe with anger. Alisa, it seemed, had been watching television, fallen asleep on the couch, and had left the front screen door unlocked.

I turned with the boys and took them to the bathroom where I ran some warm water and began getting them ready to bathe. I removed my older son's T-shirt and shorts and set him in the shallow, warm water. I turned to my younger son and removed his diaper, which was completely soiled and was sagging to his little knees. I noticed that my son had a severe diaper rash. How long had he had this rash? I felt Alisa should have been aware of this. Her job was to take care of the boys and the house. Tears ran down my cheeks as I cried for my son, who surely had been in pain but had not shown it. Had my son had this rash for so long that he'd grown accustomed to it? I had not cried since I was a young boy. I was experiencing deep feelings of love for my son and hot feelings of anger toward Alisa. How could she let our son get in this condition? I remembered suffering myself when I was young. As an infant, I had suffered from double pneumonia, and was so sick for so long, I had to learn to walk again. Apparently, my Mormon mother had not taken care of me very well, either.

I was so upset I was shaking. I began splashing warm water on the rash, which extended almost to my son's waist and down to his inner thighs. As I finished washing my sons, I lifted my older son from the tub and wrapped a towel around him. My older son enjoyed taking a bath and smiled and laughed as he played in the towel. I removed my younger son from the tub, wrapped him in a clean towel, and carried him to the boys' room. My older son followed. I finished drying my younger son and applied diaper rash cream, then put a clean diaper on him and laid him in his crib. I gently kissed him on his forehead. My younger son smiled and cooed. I finished drying my older son and dressed him in his light blue pajamas that had little carpenter tools printed on them. These were my older son's favorites because the tools on them were like Daddy's.

I heard Alisa stir. I put my older son into bed and kissed him goodnight hoping he might take a nap. I then closed my eyes, took a deep breath, and went into the living room. I looked at Alisa as she rubbed her eyes and stood up. I pulled out my buck folding hunter knife. My blood was boiling, and my mind was spinning, thinking of all the awful things that could have happened. My sons could have been lost, kidnapped, or run over by a vehicle and killed. I was shaking uncontrollably.

"You're home early," Alisa said warily. She could see that I was angry.

Her eyes drifted to the knife in my hand.

Before she said another word, I turned and stiffly walked to the TV. I looked at Alisa as I slowly reached behind the TV and unplugged the cord. With the cord still in my hand, I looped it in half, slipped the blade of the knife into the loop, and cut the electrical cord in half.

"What are you doing?" she asked in disbelief.

"Helping you keep our boys safe!" I yelled.

"What are you talking about?" she said.

"Where are the boys?" I challenged.

She looked around the living room. "They are probably in their room playing."

"You don't know where your own sons are?"

"What's going on here?" Angry and confused, Alisa was raising her voice.

"Alisa," I said, "I can't believe that you could go to sleep and let the boys wander around the neighborhood by themselves. What kind of a mother does that?" My voice was filled with fury.

I realized that my older son was standing in the hallway. I picked him up. He didn't need to witness an argument between his mother and father.

"Everything is okay, son," I comforted him. "Let's go back to bed." I carried him back to bed and laid him down, kissing his forehead. I sat with him for a few minutes.

After getting my son settled, I went back into the living room. I tossed a set of car keys to Alisa.

"Here are the keys to the El Camino," I told her. "I strongly suggest you get a hotel room for the night. I'll take care of the boys. Get what you need and get out of here now. I will try to calm down and be better prepared to discuss our situation tomorrow."

I had never hit nor harmed a woman in any way. I could hardly keep myself from doing it now.

When Alisa came home the next morning, I told her that I thought it would be best if she and the boys went to stay with her folks for a few days. I was ready to take them to the airport. "Call your parents right now," I demanded. "Make sure that it's all right with them."

Since the lumber load had not arrived, I discussed my desire to Martin. He had another crew on standby to frame this house.

CHAPTER 4

Divorce, Night School, and Wreck

I took Alisa and the boys to the airport and returned home to an empty, quiet house. It was Saturday; I had no weekend plans, and I felt as empty as the house. My mind was abuzz as I repeatedly asked myself, "What am I going to do now?" I was confused. I knew I wanted a better life than the one I'd had growing up. I had done well doing honest, hard work. I felt I needed more education. I wanted to set an example and show my sons the importance of an education. The housing industry had slowed down, primarily for the winter, and I had lost two of my three helpers. On Monday morning I discussed the work situation with Martin, who suggested I talk to Bobby, another crew leader.

I found Bobby's job site and approached him. "I could use a job, and I was wondering if I could work for you," I entreated.

"I'm sure I've got something for you," Bobby said, not wanting to pass on the opportunity to hire me. I had always managed my jobs well, and my work was superior to most.

I explained to Bobby that I was enrolled at the junior college and asked whether I might be able to take off a little early a couple of days a week to get to night classes.

"Happy to have you," said Bobby. "Be here in the morning and we'll work out a schedule for work and classes."

At home, I remembered the meditation techniques I'd learned in psychology. My mind had been racing since the incident with the boys and Alisa, and I needed some peace of mind. I acknowledged that I had not been the model husband. I had been working long hours and performing church duties. I spent what time I could with our sons. Whenever I had a free Saturday or a few rain days off, I would take the boys with me to run errands. They seemed to enjoy these outings. Once, I took them to the dump, and they were intrigued by the large trucks, front-end loaders, and mounds of trash. I did not allow them out of the truck, though, for fear it would take hours to get them back in. They also liked to run and play with me at the park. These outings gave Alisa a break.

The only social life Alisa and I had was with other Mormons. I was unquestionably faithful to Alisa. I had repented from the wild life I had lived in Spearman and from the wild times I had had with the bikers. I had not had so much as a beer for quite some time. I had provided the best I could for our family. I was learning as I went. My own dad hadn't taught me anything about being a husband and father. He had been so goofy that he never taught me about life. Because he couldn't hold a job, my father had moved our family twelve times before I had graduated from high school. This constant moving and putting up with my goofy father left me confused. The one thing he tried to teach me was how to be a Mormon.

I was faithful to the Mormon religion. I wore the required temple garment underwear that I'd begun wearing when Alisa and I were married in the temple.

But the past summer had been so hot, I just couldn't handle the extra layer of clothing. I quit wearing the garments, but I lived and obeyed the Mormons' "Word of Wisdom," which instructed followers to eat healthy foods and avoid caffeine and alcohol, which were forbidden. I had followed my father's and mother's directive to find a good Mormon girl, get married, have children, and live the life as defined by the Mormon church. Even though I had been compliant with Mormon rules, I still did not feel that my parents accepted me. Everything I had been working for was now gone, and my relationship with Alisa had turned sour. She failed at doing her part, which was to take care of the house and the boys. She'd told me that she did not care to have a physical relationship, which added more stress. I didn't know how to make her happy. Things only got worse when I took the job in Dallas, and we moved from Pasadena, 250 miles away from her family.

Remembering the breathing exercise, I sat and attempted to reach a relaxed state of mind so I could meditate. I remembered the routine the best I could and did my breathing, but the 80,000 thoughts believed to pass through a human mind each a day felt more like 160,000 to me. I was a long way from mastering the relaxation technique and was unable to slow my mind. The overwhelming question was what to do now? I wondered whether I had overreacted when I'd found my toddler sons wandering in the neighborhood unsupervised, but I was certain I would never be able to trust Alisa again. My thoughts were filled with frustration, confusion, and disorder, and that was making it hard to think things through. I would not find peace for some time. I had to trust that my in-laws would oversee the raising of my sons. I knew I would probably lose my sons to the Mormon church, as my wife's parents were devout Mormons, but, I thought, it could be worse. They could be raised by Alisa alone. I was all but finished with the Mormons. I had lived the Mormon dream; it had become my nightmare, and it was far from being over.

After a few days, I contacted a divorce attorney because discussions with Alisa were going nowhere. I had tried marital counseling with Alisa and the bishop. I had also tried taking Alisa to see Professor James in an effort to work things out. Neither attempt had any positive effect. The hopeless efforts reminded me of a time my mother had blamed me for damaging the dining room table when I had been working in the fields all day with my father and hadn't even been inside the house. Just as my mother had blamed me, Alisa was now blaming me for everything that had gone wrong.

I met with my attorney to discuss custody of the children. The attorney told me that based on political pressures and historical precedents, men almost never got custody of their children. My attorney said if I had enough money, I might stand a chance, but that it would take thousands of dollars for that to happen. I was now a highly skilled laborer, but still, my income was limited. I did not have that kind of money and learned I was even worse off financially than I thought. I was shocked to learn that I was three months behind on my truck payments. Apparently, Alisa hadn't been making the payments but had been hiding the money. This made me wonder if Alisa had been saving the bill money so she could leave me. I informed the finance company that I didn't have the money to make up the delinquent payments and volunteered to return the truck as a voluntary repossession. I still had the El Camino, so I could drive to work and take care of personal business.

A few weeks passed, and I had a visit from a good friend, Royce, who was a teammate and a home teacher in the Mormon church. I missed Royce and was glad to see him. Other members of the church no longer contacted me.

"Hey, Royce, what's up? It's good to see you," I said. I needed a friend.

"I thought I would come by and see how you're doing. Are you busy?" Royce asked.

"No, I just finished dinner and the dishes; come on in and have a seat."

Royce made his way into my sparsely furnished living room and sat on the couch.

"I have heard that Alisa is gone and wanted to know that you're doing all right," he began.

"I'm doing okay. We've been having some serious difficulties in our relationship, so she and the boys are staying with her parents for the time being," I admitted.

"I have also heard that you have a girlfriend and that she has been staying with you all night," Royce said.

I was beginning to question Royce's motives.

"So what business is that of yours?" I demanded.

"You know, Leon, that is forbidden under Mormon laws and rules. You cannot have another woman around."

"Royce, I appreciate that you're interested in my well-being, but it sounds like you and some of the other brothers have been spying on me. Who sent you, the bishop? I think it's time for you to leave." I felt betrayed.

It was true that I had met a female friend at night school and that we had been spending some time together, out and out breaking Mormon law, which was grounds for excommunication. I thought about Royce and our relationship. I had attended church with Royce, played sports with him, had even traded babysitting duties with him.

A few days after Royce's visit, just before dark one evening I heard a knock on my door. Curious, because I wasn't expecting anyone, I opened the door and saw someone walking down the steps to join a group assembled under the huge Sycamore tree in my yard.

The mob leader, shaking the Bible and Book of Mormon above his shoulder, spoke for the group. I could remember a time when my father had done the same thing, yelling at me to drive the devil out because my father hadn't liked something I had said or done.

"Brother Mecham, it is our understanding that you have been breaking the laws of the Mormon church," said the leader. "We have come to call you to repentance. If you do not repent, you will be excommunicated from the church." Each member of the mob carried a Bible and a Book of Mormon. The men were dressed in their black Sunday-go- to-meeting suits, complete with white shirts and ties. This was the Mormon Mafia! Their job was to scare, threaten, and bully people. The mob had no idea who I really was, what I was capable of, nor most of all, what I had been through physically and emotionally.

"Y'all stay right there," I said. "I'll be back in a minute." I walked to my bedroom and retrieved my Marlin lever-action carbine rifle. I remembered what my grandfather, who had been sheriff, had taught me about how to handle mobs. I walked to the front door, pushed the screen door back until it slammed against the wall with a loud bang, and stepped out onto the front porch. As the door closed behind me, I pushed the lever action forward and pulled it back, loading a Remington .35 caliber bullet into the chamber and cocking the rifle. The loaded round carried a 200-grain, round-nosed, copper jacketed lead projectile capable of taking game up to 500 pounds. It would have no trouble taking out a 200-pound Mormon or two.

"You have until the count of three to get off my property," I said as I raised the rifle to my shoulder. I settled the front sight on the left eye of the mob leader. "*One!*" The mob scattered like a bunch of roaches when a light turns on, stumbling, tripping, and almost knocking each other down. If I hadn't been so upset by their visit, I would have been rolling from laughter.

The next day, I thought about these men. These men had been my friends. How dare they call me to repentance! I knew them and knew that they had family problems of their own. The mob leader, for example, had a teenage daughter who kept running away from home, and when she was home, she refused to attend church. How is it that on Sundays these same men were preaching brotherly love, acceptance, and forgiveness? I certainly did not see love, acceptance, or forgiveness. I didn't even see anyone try to learn about or understand my side of the story. How is it that they had time to bully me or anybody else when they were not taking care of their own family business? I decided to formally announce that I renounced the Mormon church. I composed a letter, made copies, and mailed it to three different levels of leaders in the Mormon church.

"Effective today, I request that my name be removed from the records of the Mormon church. I do not care to be associated with a group of *morons* like you and want to make sure for future reference that you know you are not welcome in my house or on my property at any time."

I was not bothered again, and Royce never came back. He had obviously been spying on me and had been reporting his findings to the other members of the Mormon gossip mill.

I fell into a routine of working and going to school. Having spent my early years on a dairy farm, I had learned to begin work before sunrise and worked many a night until well after dark. I had been taught to work long hours, and with my nervous energy, I needed an outlet. Sports had always provided that extra physical challenge. I found a sort of meditation when exerting myself physically, and now more than ever, I needed all the outlets I could get.

When summer came, I had a lot of time and no classes, so in the evenings I began playing tennis. I didn't have anybody to play with, nor did I know the game. I bought a cheap racquet and a can of balls. I went to the city park and practiced ground strokes by hitting the ball against the backboard. I practiced my serve as best I could. I had been watching tennis on T.V. and had a rough concept of how to play the game. I had also gotten to know my psychology professor, Professor James, a little better and sought out his advice and counsel. I learned that Professor James played tennis. I thought the professor might teach me to play tennis.

One afternoon I spotted James on campus and mentioned that I knew he played tennis.

"I'd like to learn to play," I told him. "Could you teach me the basics of the game? I would be willing to pay what I can."

The professor offered a trade of expertise. "I understand that you're a carpenter, and it just so happens that my wife and I would like to have a cedar lattice cover over our back patio. Come out to the house, and I will show you where I want it."

Later that week, I met with the professor at his home to review the job.

"I can build this for you if you will teach me to play tennis," I told the professor. "How many lessons is it worth for you to teach me tennis if I build your cover? I do the labor and you buy the materials." This seemed to be a fair trade to me.

"I'll give you ten lessons," Professor James offered.

I was eager to begin. I checked on prices, reviewed the materials cost, and Professor James gave me a check to buy materials for his new patio cover.

By now I had filed for divorce. I knew I could not trust Alisa, and in fact, based on her comments, she apparently did not want to be married to me, although she did not have the gumption to come out and say it. She told me that she wanted to come up to get the rest of the clothes for the boys and for herself. All she had taken with her were a few clothes. I had no problem with that, and we agreed on a day for her to come get her things. I didn't want to see Alisa, so I left the house. She could get what she needed and leave.

On the agreed-upon day, I went to work. I had asked Alisa to leave her key to the front door inside the house. After work I came home to a surprise. The house was virtually empty. I slowly walked through the house, assessing what she had taken. There was not a stick of furniture in the house, not even a lamp. I went into the garage. There was no washer, no dryer, even the spare refrigerator was gone. I then went into the kitchen, where I found there was not even one spoon, knife, or fork, nothing to cook with or eat with! I went into the bedrooms, where there were no beds, mattresses, no bed covers, nothing left but my clothes and my rifle in the master closet. Even the curtains were gone. What would Alisa need with kitchenware, washer and dryer, or curtains? She was staying with her parents in their fully furnished home. My house had been stripped bare. What in the hell did she want with all the furniture? I knew her family had a washer and dryer, so why the hell did they take everything? Obviously, she had had a lot of help robbing me of what should have been half mine. Her father (a high priest in the Mormon hierarchy) had to have been the leader of this bunch. This man had been ordained to the exalted office of High Priest. He was a hypocrite who preached brotherly love, acceptance, and forgiveness but did not try to instill this in his daughter, and in fact, helped her take things she didn't need just so she could hurt her soon-to-be ex-husband.

I could get along with little to nothing as long as I had food, water, and some clothes. At least they left the house and the roof on it. If they had been able to move the house, they probably would have taken it, too. I was glad it still had doors that locked. There wasn't anything left to steal, though. Everything was now in Alisa's parents' home in Pasadena.

My attorney prepared me for divorce court and instructed me to make a list of our assets and liabilities.

On the appointed court date, I arrived at the courthouse and met briefly with my attorney. We entered the courtroom and sat down. As the judge entered, we and everyone else in the courtroom were instructed to stand. A female judge entered and positioned herself in front of the group.

"Oh Christ, I'm really going to get burned now," I said to my attorney.

"Leon, settle down; let me handle this," he said.

As the judge read from her paperwork, my mind was racing.

"Ms. Mecham, it says here that you have all the furniture and all the furnishings to the house, including the curtains."

"Mr. Mecham, it says here that you have assumed the mortgage, the cars, and all the bills, is that correct?"

"Yes, your Honor."

"Ms. Mecham, do you have a job?"

"No, your Honor."

"Where are you currently living?"

"I am staying with my parents in their home."

"Do you work?"

"No, your Honor."

"It says here that you have possession of all the furniture and household items. Is that correct?"

"Yes, your Honor."

"Ms. Mecham, are you looking for work or other living accommodations?"

"No, your Honor. I do not plan to work, and I plan to remain living with my parents indefinitely."

"Ms. Mecham, with no job and living with your parents, what do you need with all the furniture and furnishings?"

Pointing to me, Alisa said, "He told me to come and get my belongings. I took what I felt was mine. He is working and can buy his own stuff."

The judge turned to me: "Mr. Mecham, you are to make a list of all the furniture and furnishings you feel would be equitable and would like to get back and provide that list to the court for review and approval, do you understand?"

Ms. Mecham, Mr. Mecham is awarded the right to pick up all the things that are approved by this court, and you are to allow him to come and get them, do you understand?"

"Yes, your Honor."

The judge continued speaking to Alisa, "If you are not going to work and help pay for things, then you have no right to ask Mr. Mecham to pay for everything after you took everything and are not assuming any of the bills. Ms. Mecham, you are to adjust your schedule so Mr. Mecham can retrieve those things that have been awarded to him; do you understand?

"Mr. Mecham, you are to pay child support monthly and are free to retrieve those things you want convenient to your schedule."

"Thank you, your Honor," I said.

I had, in fact, offered for Alisa to continue to live in our house and had offered to pay the house payment and all the bills so my boys would be near me, but Alisa really wanted to go back home and live with her mother. She had not adjusted to being married and mostly did not like being away from her mother. I could not see that Alisa was not maturing in responsibility, only in age. At her parents' house, she would not have to clean the house, prepare meals, or take care of the boys. Her mother would do that.

I had to arrange a day to drive five hours to my former in-laws' home and retrieve eating ware, furniture, and various belongings that neither Alisa nor her family had any use for. I also had to rent a trailer to haul the stuff in. When I arrived and began loading my things, the tension was palpable. While I felt a full range of emotions, I kept most of it to myself.

I went back to my single life and paid a visit to Professor James; I had a couple of tennis lessons left. He told me I was learning quickly and that he wanted to take me to his country club, where he said someone was always looking for a match.

I'd never been to a country club, but I thought it would be a fun adventure.

At the country club, the parking lot was loaded with Cadillacs, Lincolns, Mercedes Benzes, BMWs, and a Porsche or two. I was as impressed as I was depressed. How the hell could I afford the dues to hang out with these millionaires when I could barely eke out a living and pay child support? James introduced me to the club manager, who greeted me like royalty and gave me a complete tour of the place, including the locker room, where I saw a poker game in progress and a lot of hundred-dollar bills on the table. One player had a .45 Colt 1911 on the table. I had never seen so many luxury cars and so much cash. I must have looked like I felt — like a country bumpkin.

Despite my bumpkin status, I was getting better at tennis, and Martin learned that I liked to play. He and two other crew leaders had been playing a match every Friday afternoon, but the fourth person, Martin's cousin, had bailed on them, so they needed a fourth player to commit. I was overjoyed and excited to become the fourth player, even though I was the weakest player of the group. This would give me something to do on Friday evenings besides sitting around worrying about my home situation and my future.

I worked every day I could, including Saturday and Sunday, as I had little else to do. No way in hell was I going to attend another meeting with a bunch of Mormons.

I took off one weekend to visit my mother, father, and younger brother. My little sister was living elsewhere with her fourth husband by this time. She had gotten involved in drugs, had gotten breast implants, and become a prostitute to finance her drug dependency. She had been incarcerated several times for drugs and prostitution but had finally straightened out her life, at least for the time being. My younger brother, never much of a self-motivator, was on disability and welfare. Though he was ostensibly unable to work, he would go joy riding on his ATV over rough terrain. I acknowledged that people make mistakes, and I tried to accept them and their ways. I figured everybody wanted the same things I did, which was to grow mentally and improve personally. I still adhered to the principles my grandfather had taught me: "'Do what you say, and say what you do.'"

I pulled into my parents' driveway and went into the house, calling out, "Anybody home?" It was late on a Friday night. My father had retired for the night, and my little brother was at his fiancé's home.

Finally, I saw Mom, and we chatted briefly before retiring for the night.

Saturday morning, I got up and found my dad cooking breakfast. I walked into the kitchen to say good morning and to see what was creating the delicious aromas. My father and I were still distant. I never forgot the way he'd treated me, and I never forgot the abuse, but I had accepted it as part of my life, and I did not hold grudges. I now also towered over my father, which made him seem small and harmless to me.

"Morning, Dad," I said.

Dad, with a sour look, glanced at me.

"The potatoes are almost done; the sausage is staying warm in the oven, and I'll scramble some eggs as soon as I get the potatoes out of the skillet," he said. "You can get the plates, knives, spoons, and forks on the table if you want."

I finished setting the table about the time Dad had finished cooking, and he put the food on the table. My brother and mom came into the kitchen and sat down, and Dad said a prayer over the food. The morning seemed almost too normal. I was waiting for the other shoe to fall. It didn't take long.

"Leon, how are you doing?" Dad asked companionably.

"Work is good for now," I said, "and I'm attending night school to further my education. I've learned how to read blueprints, cut roofs, and have been running a crew and framing houses."

"And how are Alisa and the boys?" my mother wanted to know.

"I don't know; I hardly speak to her."

"You know you need to repent, ask Alisa for forgiveness, and get back together," my mother advised.

"Ask forgiveness for what? I was doing my part. I was working, making repairs to the house, going to school, and performing my church duties. She couldn't take care of the house and the boys," I countered.

"You could have helped her more," Mom insisted.

"Mother, the relationship has gone way too far south to get it back." I was adamant.

Then my father chimed in: "Your mother is right. You need to repent and take care of your family."

"Have you not been paying attention to what I have been telling you all these weeks and months?" I asked, incredulous. "No way in hell am I going to take her back."

We started a heated discussion, and my blood was boiling. Nobody in the Mormon church, not even my parents, had asked me anything about my relationship with Alisa. They all had one thought, which was that I was guilty, and Alisa was an angel. My mother and father had not been willing to listen to anything I had to say.

Why should I have expected more? I had been only a farmhand to them. When Dad had a heart attack from ingesting illegal drugs he had smuggled into the country, I had gone to work in the oil fields, laying my life on the line to support him and our family. Still, these many, many years later, they lacked the common courtesy or respect to even say thank you. I should have been used to it, but this constant disrespect made me feel like Cinderella — always getting the dirty work but never getting any praise, thanks, or love.

It was time for me to leave and drive the five hours back home.

"I have better things to do than argue with y'all about this," I told them. "You've never cared about me and obviously still don't." As I was leaving, I asked myself why I had even come. I had felt alone before. I had hoped at least my family would accept me and support me, especially during what was a troubled time for me. My parents had supported my little sister during her drug and prostitution years and still showed her love. Now they rejected me because I was no longer attending the Mormon church and had broken Mormon law by getting a divorce. My sister had been divorced three times, had been a drug addict, and had worked as a prostitute. And my parents had abused amphetamines, valium, and opioids. They claimed they needed their drugs. But if I did anything they disagreed with, I was at fault and constantly told I needed to change my ways. I never lived up to my parents' expectations. Once, Mother asked me when I was going to start acting like a normal human.

All I could say to her was, "I weighed nine pounds and ten ounces when I was born. I am now over six feet tall and weigh over 200 pounds. I was not normal when I was born and am not normal now. How is it that I am supposed to be normal?" She had been so obsessed with making me fit her idea of normal that she had even forced me to be right-hand dominant (and I am a natural lefty). These thoughts plagued me. I was more disturbed, angry, and troubled now than I had ever been. With sadness, I walked out the front door to my pickup and left to make the long trip home.

Back home, I had improved my skills as a carpenter and was being assigned more difficult houses to frame. I had graduated from tract houses to working on small custom homes with Bobby. I continued to improve my carpentry skills and furthered my education. I played tennis every Friday afternoon with Martin, John, and Mike. The four of us mixed up the play by changing partners and playing the ad or deuce court.

A new country club had been built near where we had been framing houses. The club needed members and was offering a discounted fee for charter members. Martin, well known in the residential construction industry and well connected, joined and brought us to the club to show us around. We all decided the introductory price was too cheap to turn down. All four of us were now card-carrying members of a country club. We all drove pickup trucks, not Cadillacs, but, by God, we could play tennis. I had been able to squeeze in a few lessons with a professional coach here and there. I continued to improve my skills, and John and I became partners, playing doubles together. The country club's tennis championship tournament was coming up, and John and I signed up as partners. Martin and Mike had teamed up and signed up for the championship tournament, too. Mike and Martin lost in the second round, but John and I made it to the finals and found that we were pretty much evenly matched with the opposing team. It was shot for shot, serve for serve. Each team won a set. The third set had been tied at six games to six games, and we were going to the tiebreaker for the club championship! The other team was really good, but I had been able to drive nearly all of my forehand shots down the line for winners, as I was playing deuce court. I really had my forehand zeroed on that day. On occasion I would hit it down the middle to keep the other team off balance. John had mishit his return of a service shot, and the other team took advantage with a killer shot down the middle. Advantage point for the other team. On the next point I anticipated the shot and set up. I attempted to feign a shot down the middle and drive another forehand down the line. Damn, the other guy anticipated correctly, stepped onto the outside line, and volleyed the ball crisply down the middle, and they won the match. We could not have been more evenly matched. I felt successful, even though my shot had been the one picked off for a win by the other team. I felt I had played almost flawlessly throughout the match. I felt victorious, although John and I took second place. The match could have just as easily gone our way.

With my sons being five hours away and my relationship with Alisa and her family being so strained, I found it difficult to visit my boys. Every conversation I had with Alisa was filled with resentment and anger. I had grown to despise Alisa and her family after they had picked the house cleaner than a rib bone. I saw that act as demonstrating extremely poor character. But I managed to swallow my pride and keep my rage down to a simmer when I'd go to pick up the boys. I saw the boys every two or three months, especially during April, their shared birthday month, and near Christmas time. I wanted them to feel special on their birthdays and at Christmas, so I'd take them shopping and let them choose two or three presents each. I felt that by doing this, they would at least get something they wanted and liked.

It was time for me to get the boys for a visit. I called Alisa, who said that I could get the boys on Saturday morning but that I'd have to have them back by Saturday afternoon so they could attend a church function.

That would give me only a few hours with the boys. Church always seemed to be an excuse to keep me from my sons. Even with my child support payments current, Alisa would come up with reasons I couldn't get the boys — and her excuses were always church activities. Mormons do not hang out with non-Mormons. Non-Mormons are poisonous to faithful members. Non-Mormons are considered sinful, possessed by the devil, and a bad influence. I was a non-Mormon; therefore, in the eyes of my parents, her parents, and Alisa, I was possessed by the devil and was a bad influence on the boys.

One summer day I called Alisa.

"I would like to pick up the boys and bring them back here for a week. I can pick them up on Friday night and bring them back a week from Saturday," I told her.

"Be sure two bring two months' worth of child support for this month and next month," Alisa demanded. I bit my tongue. I had learned before the divorce that I could not trust Alisa, but I believed that the boys would be at least safe being raised in their grandparents' household. Alisa had been staying with her parents since our split, and she was showing no signs that she wanted to do anything else. At least the boys would not miss any meals or go to bed hungry as I had done so many times when I was growing up. I still harbored ill will toward Alisa and her family for how they had treated me. I despised her for letting our children play in the street, for stealing the money for the truck payments, forcing me to relinquish my nearly new pickup. But I saw this behavior as typical for Mormons. My experience was that if one is not a Mormon, then one doesn't exist. It seemed to me that Mormons obey the Ten Commandments only when dealing with other Mormons — and then not all the time. I had seen Mormons treat other Mormons despicably, too.

I drove five hours, picked up my boys, and drove five hours back home. We got to my house at about 2 a.m. The boys slept all the way home. They were getting older and beginning to develop some character. They both always seemed to be a little distant toward me, but I just figured that was because I had not been able to spend as much time with them as I wanted to. I had been dating a woman, Jeanette, who also had young boys, and we had planned on spending some time together, letting the boys get to know one another. All went well as the weekend and week passed. The boys and I seemed to get a little closer. I took them home to Alisa on Saturday as I had promised.

When I got back home, I called Jeanette, who had invited me for dinner. As we were eating, Jeanette said, "Leon, did you know your boys are being taught that you are possessed by the devil?"

"What?" I was stunned.

"Your ex-wife, her brothers, and others are telling your boys that you are possessed by the devil," Jeanette repeated.

"That explains why they were a little standoffish," I said.

Alisa and the good Mormon family I had married into were now sabotaging my relationship with my boys. I had hoped my sons would reach their own conclusions about Mormonism as they grew older, and maybe they would understand. But I could only hope for the best at this point. When I thought of my ex-family, I saw red. My immediate family was not much better, as they treated me worse than they would treat an unwanted stepchild. They all had shunned me. Years later, when my parents died, I learned that they had left me out of their will, also.

Burdened by my situation, I started drinking beer again, though I wasn't overdoing it. Occasionally, on a Friday or Saturday night I would drink as much as a six-pack or two to try to relax. Between attending night school, visiting a bar now and then, and playing tennis, I had no problem finding dates. I fit the bill of the tall, dark, handsome guy, and the women seemed to be drawn to my crystal blue eyes and long lashes.

In an effort to gain mental peace, I had tried meditation off and on, but I had been unable to master it. Having so much on my mind it made it doubly difficult. I could not calm my mind and allow myself to listen.

I remembered the feeling of freedom I'd felt when I rode motorcycles. A friend, Jimmy, had a Harley, but there was no way I could afford a Harley. Then, by accident, I came across a 1966, 650 cc

Bonneville Triumph. It was so cheap, I thought, if I sold a couple of things and cut a few expenses, I could have another bike. I really liked having the wind in my face and the feeling of freedom when I was riding. Maybe that was the therapy I needed. I felt guilty but bought the bike anyway.

I called Jimmy. "What are you doing this weekend?" I asked.

"Nothing, why do you ask?" Jimmy was curious.

"I just bought a used Triumph."

Jimmy suggested we take a ride. We met at his place the following Saturday and set our sights on riding to Dallas. Jimmy had grown up in the Dallas area, and he knew a few places we could ride to.

Jimmy was riding in front on his Harley Sportster, and I followed behind on my Triumph. I had had my bike in the shop at the Triumph dealership just a few days earlier to get a couple of repairs made, one of which was to fix a faulty kickstand that had a weak spring. A time or two, I had to get the kick stand up while I was riding, as it had a tendency to drop down when I went through a dip or hit a bump in the road.

We made it to a bar, where I enjoyed the energy, music, and one cold beer. We decided to leave, ride a little, and stop at another bar.

As we were riding north, we hit a dip at an intersection, and the kickstand came down! I immediately was aware of the situation and tried to get the kickstand back up, but there was a crown in the road, which made it impossible for me to get the kickstand up. As a last-ditch effort, I leaned to the right to take the weight off the kickstand, and as I kicked the stand with my left foot, I made contact with the tall, concrete curb.

My right foot was off the foot peg and was sandwiched between the peg and the twelve-inch concrete curb. The impact almost ripped my big toe off my right foot and vaulted me into the air. As I was flying down the line of the curb, I realized that I wasn't wearing a helmet. I saw telephone posts and "no parking" signs flying by my head. I raised my arms and wrapped them around my head, knowing I'd have to roll out of it. I had been taught this move in football, and I followed through with this last-second plan. I gathered myself into the fetal position with my arms around my head and landed on the pavement on my left shoulder. I skidded and rolled to a stop.

As I rolled, the pavement chipped the bones on my hips and elbows. I stared up into the starry night sky and thought, "I'm alive." Then Immediately after, "Damn, I hurt." I lay there for a few seconds.

In his rearview mirror, Jimmy had seen me flying through the air and had turned around a few hundred feet from me. Almost immediately after I landed, the car behind me stopped, and a man got out. He ran up to me and knelt down, placing his hand on my inner thigh. He asked if I was all right, but he kept rubbing my thigh. He made me very uncomfortable.

"Jimmy!" I yelled. "Get this son of a bitch away from me!"

Jimmy got to me quickly and told the man to leave, that he had everything under control.

Jimmy called an ambulance, which arrived in only a few minutes.

I asked Jimmy to get my bike home and to call Cassidy, my girlfriend. My bike was mangled. It looked like it had been dropped off a three-story building. It was a pile of twisted and bent metal. I would have to see to it later.

The paramedics asked me my name and a few other things to determine whether I was aware and able to think. They examined me and determined that I could be moved. I was put on a stretcher and loaded into the ambulance. The paramedics prepared me for the ride to the hospital.

"Which hospital do you want to go to?" the paramedic asked as he secured me into the back of the ambulance.

"My doctor is on staff at General Hospital in Grand Prairie," I responded.

The driver radioed his dispatcher to report which hospital we were heading to.

We had driven for a few minutes when the dispatcher contacted the driver, who told me the message: "We just got word that we cannot go outside Dallas city limits," he said. We were headed west on Interstate 30. "Is there another hospital in the Dallas city limits where we can take you?"

"My girlfriend has been informed that I am going to General Hospital," I said, "so I want you to take me there. Call General Hospital and see if they have an ambulance they can send to pick me up at the city limit."

The paramedic made those arrangements, and an ambulance from General Hospital met us at the city limit sign on the westbound side of Interstate 30.

We arrived at General Hospital, and someone called my physician. I was placed on a gurney parked in the hallway. It was Saturday night, and all the victims from bar fighting, car wrecks, and domestic violence had shown up. The emergency room was very busy, but I finally got my turn. I was rolled into x-ray.

As my doctor approached, he asked, "Well, what have you done to yourself?"

"Just had a little bike malfunction," I said.

"Glad it wasn't a major malfunction," the doctor said, trying to lighten the situation.

"X-rays show that your left shoulder has been dislocated, and you have four cracked ribs. You also have a dislocated big toe. We are going to have to cut your right boot off to reset your toe. Is that all right?" The doctor was very aware of the relationship we Texans have with our boots.

"Doc, these are custom-made boots and are my favorite boots of all time. Can you cut my boot so it can be repaired?" I was entreated.

"We'll do our best," he promised.

He gave me another injection for pain and a prescription to fill. About this time, Cassidy arrived. We had not been dating long. We had met at night school and had hit it off.

"Doc, I don't have hospitalization insurance. How soon can I be released?" I was concerned.

"You can go as soon as we get your shoulder and big toe put back in place, and everything else checks out."

I asked Cassidy to take me home when I was released.

"I'll take you to my apartment," she said. "Your shoulder, ribs, and foot are injured. You will be better off with a little help for now."

I didn't feel like arguing and just dropped it. Maybe it would be okay to allow someone to do something for me for a change. I wondered if I would have to pay a price for this, too. In my experience, when someone did something for me, they expected something in return.

"Thanks, I should be ready in a few minutes," I said with hope but little optimism.

"Let's get this over with, Doc. I'm ready to get out of here."

On the courts at age 40. I was ranked a level 5; level 7 is considered pro.

CHAPTER 5

Drugs and Work

The doctor had given me pills — opioids, for pain — when I first arrived at the hospital, but I was getting no relief. After my doctor had completed his examination and concluded that I was generally in good shape, despite a few cracked and chipped bones and a lot of bumps and bruises, he gave me an injection for the pain. The strength and intensity of the drug, which was probably morphine, gave me immediate relief. The doctor called the hospital custodian to get the correct tool needed to cut off my boot. The doctor used a saw-like tool to cut the seam up the side of the boot and peeled it back to remove it. When the doctor reset my big toe, I felt a strong, sharp pain shoot from my toe all the way up my leg. The pain was brutal — it was as if I'd taken nothing for pain. The doctor released me from the hospital and gave me a few more pills to take with me and a prescription for opioids for pain management.

The staff helped me into a wheelchair and got me out to Cassidy's waiting car. Cassidy helped me get into her green Pinto. Thank God, with the shoulder and toe pain not so sharp anymore, the morphine was working, and I was able to get my large frame into her econo-my-sized car.

She drove slowly and made it to her apartment. She helped me out, offering me her shoulder to lean on as I limped up the two flights of steps to her place. The short walk exhausted me. I offered to sleep on the couch, but Cassidy insisted I use the bed. With her help, I managed to get to her bed, grateful for the morphine's effect. Cassidy checked on her two girls in the second bedroom, returned to her room, changed into an oversized T-shirt, and got into bed with me.

In the middle of the night, I awoke. I'd gotten my legs tangled in the sheets, and with my ribs and shoulder throbbing, I couldn't get myself untangled. I called Cassidy.

She got out of bed, turned on a lamp, and came to my side, asking how she could help. She pulled the covers back and helped me straighten my legs. I was embarrassed, as Cassidy and I had only recently met and had been on only a few dates.

I gasped for breath as pain shot through my ribs and shoulder. The morphine was wearing off.

"Would you mind getting me a glass of water and a couple of those pain pills?" I asked.

"Not at all," said Cassidy.

Cassidy opened the brown bottle and shook two pills onto her palm.

"Here you are. Anything else I can get you?" It was 2 a.m., and Cassidy didn't seem to mind helping me. I was grateful.

"You're an angel," I told her. "Thank you for helping. I'm hoping these pills will kick in, and I will be able to get some sleep." Thanks to the opioids, I was able to drift off and sleep.

The next morning, Cassidy went to my house and got a few of my necessities. When she got back, I was sleeping. It was a Sunday, so I'd have the day to recuperate. With the help of pain pills, I slept most of the day.

I called Bobby that night and told him what had happened. I told him I'd need a couple of days off.

"Sure, buddy. Take care of yourself." Bobby agreed.

I continued to rest and kept taking pain pills.

Knowing I would not be able to work all day and go to classes at night, I canceled my enrollment at college.

By the third day after the crash, I was getting adjusted to the pain and was figuring out how to move around with my crutches. I asked Cassidy to take me home.

"Leon, I don't mind you being here," she said. "I kind of like it. If you really want to go home, I'll take you." She was a little disappointed to see me leave so soon. She had been hoping we would be able to play house for a while.

At home, Cassidy helped me get settled. I rested and took more pain pills. A couple of days later I was back on the job. I was really sore and stiff, but with no other means of income, I got up and did what I had to do. I also figured it was better working and moving around than lying in bed getting stiffer. I mostly did what little I could for a few days. After a week had passed, I was getting around fairly well and was able to move around a little without crutches. I could see, though, that full recovery would take a long time, and I'd need to adjust my lifestyle. I canceled my membership at the country club, knowing it would be a long time before I would be playing competitive tennis again.

Work was steady for the next few months, and relying on pain pills, I recovered from my injuries. My doctor, Dr. Garrett, was an osteopath. He had been a physical therapist before deciding to go to medical school. As an osteopath, he could adjust the human spine as a chiropractor would. The adjustments helped me recover from the damage to my shoulder and neck. Dr. Garrett provided all the pain pills I said I needed.

After a few months, I seemed to be back to normal, but my great toe still caused me a lot of pain. My ribs had healed, but my shoulder and upper back continued to aggravate me. I did as my doctor advised and continued to take opioids for pain. By now, I was addicted to opioids but didn't realize it. I slowly continued to get better. My doctor continued to prescribe as many opioids as I asked for. The pain would not go away.

Work was going well. I had left Bobby's operation to strike out on my own. One day as I was framing a house, I saw a new El Camino pull up to the site. A well-dressed gentleman got out and approached me.

"Are you the crew leader?" he asked.

"Yes sir," I said, extending my hand and introducing myself.

"I'm Roy Wade," he said. "How long have you been on this job?" Mr. Wade knew the answers; he was only checking my integrity.

"Let's see," I answered, "we started this job last Thursday, so we have been framing this house for about five days. I think we'll finish it in a couple more days."

He asked if I'd be interested in framing larger houses. My interest was piqued. Mr. Wade walked over to his El Camino, and I followed. He pulled out a set of blueprints for a custom home. "Are you interested in framing custom homes like this?" he asked.

"If the pay is right, I am," I answered.

We looked at the blueprints, and I discussed pricing with Mr. Wade. I quoted him a price that was a bit higher than what I had been getting, but I thought the price was fair, given the complexity of the home's design.

He said my price was fine and asked how soon I could start.

"I should be able to start on this project next Monday, no later than Tuesday," I said.

"See you at my office on Monday morning and I will give you a set of prints." We shook hands in agreement.

I started framing houses for Mr. Wade and, with the help of my pain pills, I didn't miss a lick. I was able to work but had a hard time after hours dealing with chronic pain, so I began to wash the pain pills down with a cold beer or two. I got cortisone injections in my toe and shoulder, which helped for a week or two, but then the pain would return. I returned to my doctor, who prescribed me even stronger doses of opioids.

I was still seeing Cassidy. She worked for a title company in Fort Worth and mentioned that she knew of a property for sale for a great price. "Would you like to look at it?" she asked.

"Sure, why not?" I said, thinking that Cassidy might have stumbled upon the information through her job, but that wasn't the case. Cassidy had been looking for property for her and me. She was thinking about marriage. The thought of marriage had not entered my mind. I had just gotten out of a bad marriage and still felt the sting and pain from it.

I managed to keep up my responsibilities on the job and keep up with my boys. Occasionally, I took time out on Friday or Saturday night to date. I postponed school; there was still too much pain, and the drugs were talking to me, telling me I was in pain and needed to take more.

I was occasionally invited to parties. There was always beer around and sometimes whiskey or tequila. There was usually marijuana, too, and on rare occasions, cocaine, which was offered to a few select guests. I took a friend with me to one party.

"Luke," I asked him, "do you know where I could purchase a little pot?" I found that marijuana helped me relax and left no hangover.

"I'll make a call tomorrow and see if I can find some," Luke promised.

I wanted to self-medicate. I noticed that at the parties where pot was being used, there was never any fighting or disagreements, — just relaxed people and a lot of laughter. I had made a few friends but mostly kept to myself. I feared that others would judge me harshly and reject me because of my dysfunctional family and my past Mormon affiliations. But I needed friends during this time, and I was making more connections with people who smoked pot and used cocaine.

Being in the circle of people who used drugs, I learned about a new drug called crystal. Snorting crystal, an amphetamine, was snorting harsh chemicals through one's nose. These chemicals burned and stung the interior of one's nostrils. If a person snorted a little too often, it would make the inside of his nose raw and bloody. And taking an overdose or getting some poorly cooked product could be fatal. I wasn't sure I wanted to live anyway, so what the hell? I was game to try it. The usual procedure for snorting coke or crystal was to put some product on a small mirror, chop it up with a razor blade, then roll up a hundred-dollar bill, and use the currency as a snorting tube. I did not usually have a hundred-dollar bill, so when I was called on, I usually used a one-dollar bill. The rule of thumb was, if you didn't have a hundred-dollar bill, then you couldn't afford the drug. I didn't care what the rule was, I was in no mood to put up with such rules; I was only too happy to try something different to ease my emotional and physical pain.

Cassidy seemed to be okay with everything I did, but she began pushing a little harder for marriage.

I respected Cassidy a lot and might have even been a little in love with her, but no way in hell was I ready to tie the knot again. Cassidy even spoke of having children together. I was in no position to think about marriage, much less fathering more children, so I tried to break it off peacefully with Cassidy. Instead, we had a lovers' quarrel, which created more hurt and rejection. I began thinking that death was not such a bad thing. I owned a .357 Magnum, Smith and Wesson. All I had to do was cock it, put the barrel into my mouth, and pull the trigger. It would be over instantly.

Despite these thoughts, I kept my daily routine and handled my work responsibilities. One day while I was on the job, a vehicle pulled up, and a well-dressed man approached me.

"Are you the boss?" he asked.

"I guess you could call me that. What can I do for you?" I responded.

"I need some office buildings built. Is this something you can do? Would you be available to help on that kind of a project?" he inquired.

"How much are you paying?" I wanted to know.

"Let's look at the blueprints; I am sure we can come up with something equitable," he said.

Not only had I become competent, but I had also earned a reputation for being a highly skilled carpenter who produced a nearly flawless product. I loved my job and most particularly I loved the smell of wood and fresh sawdust. Even though I was either drunk or stoned and sometimes both most of the time now, I had established myself and made a name for myself in the home-building community. I could walk around the skeleton of a fully framed house, and when the walls were raised — to a height that ranged from 8 feet to 10 feet high — I would walk the top plate, which was only three and a half inches wide. I walked the plates to lay out and mark for ceiling joists, rafters, and/or prefabricated trusses. Not only could I walk the plates, I could do it frontward, backward, stoned, drunk, or both. My work was about the only thing I cared about, and I took great pride in it. I continued to frame small office buildings, custom homes, and even a tract home here and there to fill in my schedule. I ran the crew during the day, and in the evening, I would install exterior sheathing or decking on the houses I had framed. I needed all this physical exercise to work out the psychological pain I was suffering from. It exhausted me, so I managed to get some semblance of a good night's sleep, but my sleep was not very peaceful nor restful.

One day an old acquaintance dropped by.

"Leon, dang it, how are you doing?" he asked.

"Damn, Dicky, it's been a long time," I greeted him. Dicky was never my favorite person, but he did have his humorous moments, and he was a pretty good carpenter. I had worked for and learned from Dicky and Jody.

"I have some blueprints for a sorority house near the University of Texas at Arlington. It's too big for me and my crew; would you be interested in partnering up for this project?" he asked. "I don't carry workman's compensation insurance, do you? We will need to provide proof of insurance to get this job."

I told him that I did carry workers' comp and could provide the documentation.

We looked at the prints together and decided to move forward with framing the large, two-story project. This was a sorority house near the University of Texas at Arlington campus. Even as skilled as I was, this size of a job really required more manpower than I had access to and certainly more than Dicky had. This was also a some-what high-profile job and would be great to have on my resume. I had recently been a major player in the remodel of the telephone office downtown, and I continued to get recognition in the community and establish my presence, despite my drug and alcohol dependency.

My doctor was the only one who knew of my drug abuse, although Cassidy had questioned me a time or two. I kept beer in my cooler for after work, but I had started having my first beer at about 9 a.m. and would keep drinking until bedtime or until I passed out after I got home. I'd take a few pain pills here and there, and on occasion I would buy some pot.

I told Dicky that I needed to take a four-day weekend, as the Fourth of July was coming up, and I'd made plans to attend a Willie Nelson concert.

"You've been working hard, and you deserve some time off," Dicky said. "Go ahead; I can hold down the fort while you are gone."

When I got back to town on Monday, I learned that Dicky had persuaded the builder to make out the weekly draw in his name, thereby cheating me out of a couple of thousand dollars. I had been carrying the liability insurance, so I thought I was in charge of the money. I contacted the builder and argued with him until he agreed to cancel one check and cut another check to help me out. He also contacted his bank. Dicky had forged my signature on another check, but it was too late to correct that one. I would have to make up the deficit. Not wanting to face me after stealing from me, Dicky left the job. This gave me the opportunity to finish the large project alone. It was nearing completion, and I finished it with my small crew. The whole experience lifted my reputation further, as the builder saw my integrity and Dicky's lack of it.

Not long before the job was finished, I'd injured my wrist in a skateboarding accident, but the injury didn't hinder my completing the job. A few days after the injury, I was invited to a party. I went and brought a friend. My friend and I were sitting at a counter in the kitchen when whom did I see? None other than Dicky Boy. Dicky was walking toward us but didn't see me as the place was crowded. As Dicky got closer, I slipped between a couple of people and stepped in front of him. His eyes grew larger than silver dollars. With my wrist injured, I delivered my right elbow to Dicky's face, rendering him unconscious. My friend grabbed me. "Let's get the hell out of here before the police get here," he advised.

As we left, my friend suggested I take off my cowboy shirt and cowboy hat, as the police might be looking for me. We made it to my red Chevy Dually; I put my cowboy shirt and hat into the toolbox, and we took off down a side street.

"That was almost as much fun as the concert was," I said. I ran into Dicky one other time and did the same as I'd done before. I had learned that Dicky had earned a reputation for being a thief, liar, and coward.

At work, things were slowing down. I got a call from my long-time Mormon friend, Dep. He asked about business, and I told him I was finding it hard to keep my crew busy. Dep said he knew of a contractor in Houston who was looking for dependable help who could produce high-quality work.

"I told him about you," Dep said.

I thanked him but told him I had no interest in moving back to Houston.

"Well, if you change your mind, let me know," he said.

I continued to find projects here and there to keep my crew and me busy. Winter was nearing, and we braced for an early freeze. I took on another job as a framing contractor in a different subdivision. The houses were tract homes financed by a national corporation based in Massachusetts. The superintendent over the project was from Boston. I had decided after my first encounter with him that I didn't really care for him, but I took the project on anyway. The framing load had been partially assembled in a plant. The walls were prefabbed in a plant and were ready to be put in place on site. The prefabbed walls were hauled in on a flatbed behind a semi-truck. Basically, this system was a paint-by-numbers project. One of the problems that I faced was that the load had been damaged in shipping and needed a lot of extra work to repair the damage.

I alerted Ivy, the superintendent, explaining that the load would need repair.

"There are some two-by-fours, studs, and other pieces of lumber that you can use to repair the damage. Use your pickup and haul whatever you need from the lumber pile over there by the job shack. Keep up with your time, and I will see that you get compensated," he promised.

I proceeded with the project and completed numerous repairs to the damaged walls. I submitted an invoice for part of my earnings. I had used my pickup to haul materials and had to pay my laborers to help me move the lumber to the project and to make the needed repairs.

I was stunned when I got my check. "Ivy, this check is way short of what I turned in; what's going on?" I questioned.

"I know it's short," Ivy conceded. "You need to get this project completed, and I'll get it all together and get you paid."

This concerned me because I was typically paid each week so I could pay my crew and expenses.

The weather had turned cold. It had been raining, and a flu epidemic had been affecting my crew. Those who could work and I had been keeping a fire burning in a fifty-five-gallon drum near the house so we could warm up our hands and feet every once in a while.

It was muddy, cold, and wet. My crew and I were able to complete the job, and I asked Ivy to inspect the framing so he could sign off on the work completed.

My crew had left for the day, and Ivy came to inspect the project. He was nit-picking the job. I had a lot of experience, and I quickly saw what he was doing. He had set me up to frame this house and fix the damaged load. He never intended to pay for all the extra time we spent to make the repairs Ivy said he would pay for.

"Ivy, this is bullshit, you have an invoice for work I have completed, and I need to get paid," I told him.

Ivy turned to walk away, laughing and saying he would not pay and that there was nothing I could do about it.

I just thought about my crew who did the work. Ivy wasn't going to pay me, and I would still have to pay my crew. I was livid.

I turned and walked along with Ivy as we headed in the general direction of my pickup. I got slightly ahead of Ivy and opened the passenger door to my pickup and lifted my 20-gauge sawed-off pump shotgun off the gun rack. I turned toward Ivy.

"I would appreciate it if you paid me what you owed me, now!" I demanded.

"F*** you, I'm not paying you," Ivy said, his eyes twinkling and laughing at me.

I laid the barrel of the Mossberg 20-gauge pump on the side of Ivy's left hip, pushed the safety off, and pulled the trigger, discharging the 20- gauge shotgun into the dirt. *Boom!* Ivy's eyes lit up and grew as big as dinner plates. I could not contain my rage. I drew back the shotgun and swung the butt end upward, making contact with Ivy's chin, effectively breaking his jaw in two places. Ivy had been lifted off his feet and, in the air, he spun around from the blow and landed face down in the mud. I put the end of the shotgun barrel on the back of Ivy's head.

"I should kill you right now, you lying, thieving, Yankee bastard," I said, emptying the spent shell and loading another live round. I knew it was going to be bad for me, but I kept my senses around me the best I could, despite the effects of my emotions, the drugs, and alcohol. For some reason, I reached down and picked up the spent shell and tossed it into the bed of my pickup. I slid the safety button back into the safe position with my thumb and put the shotgun back on the gun rack in my Dually. I did not know what to do, so I got into my pickup and started for home with no plan in mind. As usual, I had been drinking and using my prescription pain medication. I was stoned and drunk.

I made it fewer than three miles when I turned the corner and saw more police cars in front of me than I had ever seen in one place. I stopped immediately. Some of the officers were out of their cars with their doors open and had their pistols, shotguns, and rifles aimed in my direction. Over the loudspeaker I heard, "Put your hands in the air and get out of your vehicle slowly."

I put my left hand out the open window with my fingers spread wide as I opened the door with my right hand. I moved a few steps away from my pickup, raised my right hand into the air, making it obvious I was unarmed, and I slowly knelt down.

"Lay face down on the ground and put your hands behind your back!" an officer yelled.

I put my hands on the ground and eased myself down until my face was on the black asphalt.

An officer ran forward to me. Sharp pain radiated through my back as the officer pressed his knee into me when he cuffed me. I was arrested and taken to jail. My shotgun was confiscated.

At the police station, I was fingerprinted, and my personal property was tagged and bagged. Before I was taken to a cell, I was allowed one phone call, so I called an attorney. I had provided some assistance to this attorney's office a couple of years before, when I was going to night school. I had helped put out political signs as part of a public service effort and a school project. One of the young attorneys took the call and told me he would be at the jailhouse within the hour. It seemed as though the attorney arrived just as the officer closed the door to my cell.

"Okay, Leon, I know the judge personally, and you are released into my custody. We have a party going on at the office; let's go," the attorney said.

I collected a large brown envelope that held my wallet and other items I had been carrying before this fiasco. The police would not release my shotgun.

I rode with my attorney to his office and was invited to stay awhile and have a drink or two. I stayed a bit and had a beer before calling a friend to help me retrieve my pickup. We got the truck from where it had been towed to, and I made my way home.

"What the hell am I going to do now?" I thought. I was worried that I would go to prison for breaking Ivy's jaw, though I felt justified for doing it and would probably do it again. I had sold my house and had invested the equity in a couple of vacant building lots. I had to finance the balance, and I would eventually lose all my investment. I did not owe much else, as I had moved into a small, inexpensive apartment, and aside from child support, I had only the rent and my pickup payments to make.

With all these thoughts circling, I finally fell asleep that night. The next morning, a Saturday, I called Dep.

"Hey, Dep. It's Leon. Is that contractor in Houston still looking for some help?" I asked.

"I'm not 100 percent sure, but I think he will put you to work. What's going on.? Why the change in attitude?" Dep asked.

"Work is really slow here, and I need a job," I told only a partial lie, a lie by omission. I really did need a job. I felt I needed to get away from the area. If word got out about the incident, it would be difficult to get work. All of a sudden, Houston didn't seem so bad.

"Come on down," said Dep. "I have some work that will keep you busy for a few days, and that will give you an opportunity to meet the owner of the contracting company."

"I'll be leaving early Monday morning," I said. "I should be there around noon. I'm looking forward to seeing you again."

I arrived in Houston and called Dep. I told him I was staying at my parents' house in La Porte. Dep was among the friends from the Mormon group I had associated with in Houston years before. Dep had never been judgmental toward me. I felt at times that Dep was the only real friend I had in the world. I was grateful I had at least one.

Dep instructed me to meet him at San Jacinto Junior College at seven the next morning.

I helped Dep and his crew put a roof coating on a building at the junior college where I had taken some classes a few years before. We completed the project in a couple of days, and Dep had another project or two for me to help with. Dep paid me fairly and told me he had spoken with the general contractor. He told me how to contact him.

I made an appointment to meet the general contractor at his office. The receptionist greeted me and told me that Mr. Stone was expecting me. I walked to the office at the end of the hall and opened the door.

"Good morning, Leon. Have a seat," said Mr. Stone.

I approached him, extending my hand for a shake before I sat down. I thanked him for seeing me.

Mr. Stone got right down to business.

"Leon, I have been told some good things about you and how you work. We could use some good help. We are producing about $25 million a year and need good people badly," he said.

"What are you paying, and how can I be of help to you?" I asked, getting right down to business myself. We agreed to a reasonable wage, and I agreed to start work as a carpenter foreman the next morning.

I went back to my parents' house but didn't tell them much, as I knew they didn't approve of my activities. They were still insisting that I reconcile with Alisa.

Still in some pain, I was short on medications and asked my mother, who had been taking Valium and opioids for more than twenty years, if she had some aspirin, Excedrin, or something for the pain in my shoulder and back.

"Here, take one of these," she offered.

I swallowed a pill, and a couple of minutes later, thought, "Holy crap!" This stuff was a lot stronger than what my doctor had been prescribing. It nearly knocked me out as an opioid rush came over me.

I gathered my wits and told my mother that I'd taken a job with a contractor in Houston. I asked if I could stay with her and Dad for a few days until I found a place to live. I offered to help pay expenses.

"It's all right with me, but your dad will be home around six. We can confirm it with him," she said.

When Dad got home, we discussed the situation. I was to get an apartment of my own within a few days, and while I was staying with my parents, I'd pay them rent. Things seemed to be a little calmer between my parents and me, of course I was giving them money again, but I was grateful for a place to stay. I needed a little support.

I reported for work as directed the next morning, at Houston Intercontinental Airport. The project was remodeling the Budget Rent-A-Car offices and building a forty-foot-high watch/security tower for Budget.

At the job site, I asked for and was directed to Burt, the man Mr. Stone sent me to see.

In no time, I was busy. I took on the responsibility of lead carpenter and layout man. I got into the swing of things quickly, and a few days later, the manager of the auto maintenance with Budget approached me with some information. He explained that shortly after Burt began the project, things began coming up missing. He said that on weekends, Burt and his brother had been seen hauling lumber and other things off the job site. They would bring in an empty trailer and leave with it full. He said the shop was missing tires, batteries, and about twenty-five gallons of motor oil. He also reported that Burt had loaded up concrete forming materials and had hauled them off. These materials belonged to the concrete contractor.

I thanked him for the heads-up and thought, "Oh, boy, another thief and liar. I'll have to watch myself, or I'll end up getting blamed by association if nothing else."

Shortly thereafter, Burt approached me. "Leon, we need some materials from another job; would you be willing to use your pickup and bring them over here? I'll turn in for some mileage and usage for your pickup if you will," he said.

"Okay, Burt. Make a list, and I'll go and get them," I said.

I had always been on guard, and now, I was on double guard. This was sounding too familiar.

Each week, I submitted expense reports and got paid along with my hourly wages. Then, I was working one Saturday and saw some building materials being loaded onto an empty sixteen-foot flatbed trailer that a stranger was driving. The stranger had been talking to Burt just a few minutes earlier. I decided to talk to Mr. Stone about all this. I requested a meeting. I provided the information that the Budget manager had shared with me. I also informed Mr. Stone that I did not wish to work on the project as long as Burt was on the job. I asked if there was another project I could be transferred to, and I got assigned to a burned-out school building project in South Houston.

My court date was coming up in Fort Worth, and I had to go back to the Metroplex area. I also needed to clean out my apartment in Grand Prairie and move everything to my apartment in Houston. I had been getting by on very little and was ready to get my things moved.

I explained to Mr. Stone that I needed to take a couple of days off so I could take care of some unfinished business and retrieve the remainder of my possessions.

Mr. Stone said for me to do what I needed to do; he was very accommodating to his newest and best worker.

I drove up on Thursday, as Friday was my court date. My attorney arrived at the courtroom shortly after I did. He asked, "Well it's time; you ready"?

"I guess so," I said. Neither he nor I knew exactly what to expect. My mind was racing, and I was thinking that I might even have to do some time at the Cross-Bar Hilton, the local name for the jail.

The courtroom was nearly full. My attorney and I sat on a long, wooden bench near the rear of the room.

"Ivy, Eugene vs. Mecham, Leon," the judge said. I was instructed to stand in front of the judge. Ivy was sitting near the front on the opposite side of the room. I glared at him as I passed by; I wanted to hit him again but remained stoic.

The judge read from the paper he held. "It says here that you struck Ivy in the jaw. Is that true?"

"Yes, I did, Your Honor," I admitted.

"Why would you do something like that, Leon?" Judge Delaney was reported to be about eighty years old and sharp as a tack.

"Well, Your Honor, I did a lot of work for him on the promise he would pay me for the extra work he requested that had not been in our original agreement. I had to pay my crew for the work. Once the work was complete, he refused to pay me."

"Were there any complaints on the work quality or what was done?"

"No, Your Honor. He never complained about my work."

"Ivy, was the work completed to your satisfaction?"

"Yes, Your Honor. I had no complaints on the work done."

"Why didn't you pay for the work done?"

"The company refused my request for this repair project, and I needed it done." Ivy said, looking around the room and down at the floor. He would not make eye contact with the judge.

"If you were short on cash, why did you request the additional work?"

"It was something extra I needed done."

"Did you agree to pay Leon for the additional work?"

"Yes, Your Honor."

"Did you pay him?"

"No, Your Honor."

"Well, shit, I would hit you, too, if you refused to pay me. Leon, it says you are from Missouri. Do you know where Springfield is?"

"Springfield is about seventy miles east of Joplin, Your Honor."
I was puzzled by the question.

"Well, let's see, you have been charged with assault. I'm sorry,"
he apologized, "but I have to fine you, and the minimum fine for
assault is $325. You will also have 180 days of probation."

"Your Honor, I am currently working and living in the Houston
area. Will that be a problem with my probation?"

"No. We can have you assigned to a probation officer in the
Houston area. It is also my understanding that the police took your
shotgun. It is the order of the court that the police are to return your
shotgun. After all, we cannot have a good Missouri boy running
around without his shotgun. Case dismissed." After court, I went to
the police station to retrieve my shotgun. They were not able to find
my shotgun. I decided it was part of the cost that I had to pay and
let it go.

My attorney's claim to have been friends with the judge seemed
true. I felt that it was about time I caught a break. The community
service I had performed for the government class I had taken had
paid off big time.

I rented a small trailer, cleaned out my apartment, and hauled
my remaining possessions to Houston.

Settling more permanently in Houston, I got into somewhat of
a rhythm, and by chance met a group of people who taught dance lessons. I had danced with a young woman at the Yellow Rose Country
and Western dance hall who was a part of that group. She told me
that I was a pretty good dancer and asked me if I would be interested
in taking lessons.

"I would love to take some country and Western dance lessons, but due to circumstances and financial limitations, I can't really
afford them," I told her.

Debbie said, "I really think you have some natural talent; come on by the dance studio, and we can discuss it with the manager."

A couple of days later, I met the manager, Frank. Debbie introduced us and told Frank that she had danced with me at the Yellow Rose and that she thought I had natural talent. She explained my financial situation.

"Leon, it is always good to meet a natural talent, and if Debbie says you have talent, then come on and join the group," Frank said. "Maybe your finances will improve, but in the meantime, you can contribute by helping teach some of the new students. We have a shortage of male dance teachers around here."

Damn, I got another break. Things were looking up.

I began hanging out with the instructors. We visited clubs and bars like Mickey Gilley's, The Bullwhip, and the Yellow Rose, where there was a large dance floor, and we would put on a show. Debbie and I became great partners and would show off our skills. I loved spinning and moving to the music with Debbie. She was really light on her feet and responsive to everything I asked her to do on the dance floor; she moved with ease. In turn, she helped me with my lead and steps to dances like the Texas Two Step, the Cotton-Eyed Joe, and the Schottische.

Though my lifestyle might not have shown it, I was still hooked on pain meds. I ran out of the prescription drugs I had been getting from Dr. Garrett, who was 250 miles away. Some of my coworkers on the construction jobs knew people who could supply me with various brands and types of chemicals. The drugs kept talking to me, and I was convinced I could not live without pain pills. This was the real part of addiction. The drugs talk to the patient. Not only did I find new suppliers, but also between drug buys, I began drinking a lot of

156

tequila. José Cuervo and I got really close. I developed my bartender skills and learned to make killer margaritas.

Though I now lived very close to my boys, because I was always drunk, stoned, or both, I did not improve my relationship with them. I would sober up long enough to take my boys shopping for birthday and Christmas presents but saw the boys infrequently. Despite my dependence on drugs, I managed to keep my job and still somehow perform at a high level.

I hadn't seen my family in a while, so I went to visit my parents. On this visit, I met Kimberly, who was the sister of my little brother's best friend. I was taken by her good looks. We began seeing one another on weekends. Kimberly had a job, was going to school in the evenings, and also had two children. I admired her looks and manners and was impressed that she worked and went to school. I had known her only a couple of weeks, when, drunk and stoned, I asked her to marry me. She had no idea of the condition I was in. The economy was going down in Houston and everywhere else. I'd had to change jobs a couple of times to stay employed. But she accepted the proposal, and a few weeks later, we were married by the Justice of the Peace.

I rented a nice brick home, and we moved in. I liked her two children and helped take care of them after my work hours.

One afternoon, I got home early. Kimberly, who had quit going to school, was there and told me that she had quit her job earlier that day. Her older child asked for cake and ice cream for lunch. Kimberly began getting it ready.

"Kimberly, what the hell are you doing?" I asked, incredulous. "You shouldn't be giving these kids cake and ice cream until they have had some healthy food."

"These are my kids, and I will feed them what I want to," she said. Our words escalated, and Kimberly tried to slap me in the face.

I blocked her attempt. Depressed and upset, I felt like I needed a drink. I left the house.

When I returned a couple of hours later, I saw three police cars in front of the house. I parked and got out of my pickup. I approached an officer, introduced myself, and asked what was going on.

"I have to inform you that there has been a domestic complaint, and you are not allowed to go into the house. Your wife is getting some things out of the house and will be leaving in a few minutes."

"Good Lord," I thought, "What the hell am I doing, and what have I done?"

Kimberly left, and I went into the house. She had taken only her clothes and the children's clothes and left everything else. At least she didn't clean me out like Alisa had done.

The next day I called a divorce attorney, explained the situation, and asked what it would cost to file for divorce. The marriage and divorce took about sixty days.

I realized I needed to do something. I'd had another disastrous relationship and was battling drug and alcohol addiction. I knew something had to give.

I had learned that my father had purchased a small parcel of land in the heart of Davy Crockett National Forest in deep east Texas. I called Dad.

"Dad, would you let me make camp on your property for a few days?" I asked. "I have to get away and need some time to think. I have just filed for divorce again."

He said that they would be going to the property the coming weekend. He invited me to meet them there, where we could discuss my situation.

I met with my parents at the property, and my father told me he'd bought a trailer house and parked it on the land. "There is no water nor electricity to it, but it does have a roof, and it will keep you dry if you want to sleep in there," he offered.

"Dad, I have a lot to think about, and I just need some time alone," I confessed.

"Take your time and get your life straightened out," my father advised. Then the other shoe dropped.

"I sure could use some money to purchase an old tractor and a few tools," Dad said.

I told him I'd saved some money for college and that I'd need it paid back in the fall. I asked how much he needed.

Despite my alcohol and drug dependency, I had paid off my pickup and had only a couple of other small bills. I was virtually debt free. Though I have no clue how I was able to do it, I had saved about $5,000.

"If you would loan me $3,000, I will pay you back this fall," my father promised.

I handed over a check, fighting my inclination to distrust my father. And sure enough, when fall came, there was no payback from Dad.

But he'd offered to let me stay on his and Mom's land, so I quit my job, loaded my possessions onto an old thirty-foot, tri-axle trailer I'd managed to get, and headed for Davy Crockett National Forest in east Texas near Lufkin. I was so lost, the only thing I knew was that I had to slow things down and get a grip on life. I was exhausted, hungover, and frustrated, having allowed myself to be controlled by drugs and alcohol. I had made a lot of bad decisions, and now I needed to make a good one or two. I wasn't sure how, but I had to find a way. I was over thirty years old and desperately needed to find my direction and path.

Along with my possessions, I'd brought all the drugs I had been able to purchase on the black market: opioids, quaaludes, and some amphetamines. I even had about a half an ounce of pot. I went into town and purchased a new McCullough twenty-four-inch chainsaw and a couple bottles of whiskey.

At the property, there were no neighbors for a couple of miles, and there was a lot of dense underbrush and lots and lots of pine trees. The twenty acres had been partially cleared, and there was a huge brush pile close to the trailer house. When I bought the chainsaw, I also stocked up on plenty of Southern Comfort, my preferred beverage. Every day I cut up some firewood, and every night I built a small bonfire and burned it up. I had recently purchased a Weimaraner puppy. She would go to the edge of the firelight and bark from time to time. I would get up and fire whatever weapon I had with me. I had a couple of pistols, a shotgun, and a rifle. I would shoot in the direction of Missy's bark and then go back to my picnic table and reload the firearm. I got drunk, stoned, or both every night, cut up more firewood during the day, and repeated the same routine day after day for a few weeks.

I knew I needed to find direction, and I knew I needed it immediately. I remembered my breathing exercises and began trying to relax. I carried the guilt my mother laid on me when she blamed me for all her physical problems. I carried guilt for the sins I had committed when I was working in the oil fields, from the things I did when I was running with the bikers, and now, for two failed marriages. I especially carried guilt for having abandoned my two boys because of my dependence on drugs and alcohol. I was an emotional wreck. I was considering suicide. Who gave a shit, anyway? Not my parents; my ex-wives; nor my sons, who never saw me anymore. I thought. I began meditating every evening in front of the fire as I became mesmerized by the flames. The two important questions I asked myself were simply, "Where am I going now?" and "What am I going to do with the rest of my life?" I was getting to know myself.

I spent close to three months alone in the middle of Davy Crockett National Forest. I soon ran out of drugs and chose not to buy any more alcohol. I decided to quit doing drugs and drinking alcohol altogether. I had lost about thirty pounds and was little more than skin and bones.

I had discovered a few things about myself, and I now became acutely aware of those things. I had always taken care of my family and friends, and now it was time for me to do something for myself. Through hours and hours of meditation, I found an inner strength I had never, ever felt before, and I found a resolve deep down in the marrow of my bones.

I had made quite a bit of money over the years and had been able to keep only a very small part of it. I wanted to achieve something no one could ever take away from me. I determined that I really wanted to graduate from college; that is, a major university, not some unknown college. I also resolved to learn the art of self-defense.

After ninety days of meditation, while in the forest, I had cleared my mind and found a new level of peace. I had established a direction and two goals, which I was now determined to achieve. I had quit looking back to my family history, the Mormons, and my failures. Looking back had prevented me from looking forward. Looking back had contributed greatly to my poor mental state and had only added to my confusion and frustration. When looking back, I stumbled over those things in front of me.

My mind was clear now; I was ready to go back to the real world and implement my plans.

CHAPTER 6

University and Tae Kwon Do

I decided to head to the Dallas/Fort Worth area. On my way there, I'd been wondering where I would stay while I made some decisions. I stopped to see a long-time business acquaintance and friend, who offered to let me sleep on his back porch. It was springtime, so it was perfect. I then contacted my long-time friend and tennis coach, Professor James.

After meeting with James, I visited four college campuses. I also requested my college transcripts, which were not extensive, but if they saved me from duplicating classes, wasting time, and if they saved me some money, they were worth getting. Any university would require them, anyway. I spent the next few days looking through the course catalogs, reading the requirements for various majors, and reviewing costs. I decided I'd earn a bachelor's degree in something. The college campuses I was considering were all high caliber. I didn't want an easy ride through college, and I didn't care for a pointless degree. At the same time, I was terrified by the thought that I was not smart enough to pass the classes required to graduate.

I thought of my father, who had no respect for college graduates. My father always referred to them as educated idiots. Now I want to become an "idiot"? The mistakes and decisions I had made up to this point might have defined me as an idiot, but I had met a couple of people early in my adult life who still impressed me in a very positive way, and they were educated men. Professor James, originally my teacher, and now also my mentor and friend, was certainly educated and was still earning additional advanced degrees.

I looked up some other associates and friends. I found one of them, Butch, running a crew and framing a tract home near Flower Mound.

"Hey, Butch, how are you doing, man?" I greeted my old friend and asked him if he knew where I might find work.

"Well, hell, yes," said Butch. "You can come to work right now on my crew. When do you want to start?" He was enthusiastic. I said that I could start the following Monday.

I had done all I could toward continuing my education, and I was waiting to get my college transcripts. I had decided to attend the University of Texas at Arlington, assuming I would be accepted, because it was conveniently located in the Metroplex. I knew a lot of people around there, and I knew my way around the area. Living around Dallas/Fort Worth also gave me more opportunities for work, should I need to pick up some additional money. I hoped to become a full-time student so I could finish my degree plan as quickly as possible. I was not only going to school for myself, but I believed I needed to set a good example for my boys. I wanted my sons to get an education because members of my immediate family were basically uneducated hillbillies, people with no education, no direction, and no motivation. They were just poor people with no direction; they were working, paying the bills, and basically just existing while attending all the Mormon meetings and events they could. I wanted more for my boys, and I knew I needed to start them thinking about what they wanted out of life and motivating them. Now I could provide an example; maybe that would help give them a direction.

Every chance I got, I'd ask my sons, "Where are you planning to go to college, and what are you going to study?" With the boys now nine and eleven years old, it was a distant answer to a now question. They would shrug their shoulders and look like deer caught in headlights.

I went to work for Butch, but my shoulder and back were irritating me badly with the physical nature of the work. I was hell bent on not taking pain pills, so I looked and asked around to see if there was something else available. I began spending a lot more time in meditation to help with the pain and to stay focused on my goals.

I had to find another gig quickly as the housing development we had been building was filling up with houses, and there were only a few lots left to build on.

One evening I got a phone call from James. "Hello, Leon? Are you still looking for somewhere else to live?" he asked.

"Sure am," I said. "Do you know of some place?"

He mentioned his house in Grand Prairie and said he'd rent it to me. I had been there before and was somewhat familiar with it.

James knew of my goals, needs, and financial situation. James said if I'd pay utilities, he'd rent me the house for $125 a month. That was about one-fourth the rental value of a house like that!

"Yes, sir, I'll take it," I accepted gratefully.

I had caught a huge break, and I knew it. Professor James believed in education, saw an opportunity to contribute, and was willing to provide a hand up not a handout. He had just been awarded his fifth college degree, a doctorate in educational psychology.

I wasted no time loading up my stuff and moving into my new digs. I got the rest of my things from my parents' house. I left the building materials I'd accumulated, though, because my father would sometimes use them.

I learned about a job opening from a former employee. I applied and was hired. The work was still carpentry, but it was steadier, out of the rain, and out of the sun. I was helping build the Sheraton-Lincoln Hotel at Coit Road and LBJ Freeway. This was a union job, so I had to join. I had never worked a union job before. I was now setting metal studs and hanging 5/8-inch Sheetrock. I had always enjoyed learning to use new materials and new methods. When it came to learning carpentry, my brain was like a sponge.

Because I had lost so much weight, I felt weaker than usual. I checked on a physical fitness routine at the health spa/gym in downtown Grand Prairie, although I knew little to nothing about the proper way to lift weights or to use any of the machines. One evening I was looking around the spa, and on the third floor I discovered a martial arts class.

"Can I help you?" offered the Tae Kwon Do instructor.

"I was just watching," I said.

"The best way to evaluate something is to get involved in it. Come to class a few times and see how that works for you. There are no dues or fees for a trial period. Classes are twice a week," he said.

"Nah, I couldn't do that," I demurred.

"Why not?" the instructor persisted.

"I have football knees, a wrecked shoulder, and a bad back." I enumerated my reasons for not taking a martial arts class.

"Wow, that sounds pretty bad, but I'll tell you something; in fact, I'll promise you something. If you'll attend class and do things the way I show and tell you to do them, you will overcome a lot of your back and shoulder problems and maybe even help some of your knee problems."

I was curious. The instructor explained that the martial art he taught was Tae Kwon Do and that practicing it would strengthen my muscles, which would support my back, shoulder, and knees.

"You are welcome to participate for two weeks at no cost to you," he said. "We have classes on Tuesday and Thursday evenings at seven and occasionally on Fridays."

"Thank you; I'll think about it," I answered vaguely.

"Don't think about it; come to class and try it out. If you don't like it, you can always quit," he reasoned.

I had started my new job. It was physically demanding, but I was working through a union, and the pace was slower. In fact, the tasks were sometimes more complex and required more thinking and less physical exertion.

I kept thinking about Tae Kwon Do. I was extremely apprehensive about learning new things other than carpentry. Neither my father nor mother had given me any encouragement to learn, and even some of my elementary teachers embarrassed me because of my performance. I had pretty much grown up in a barn, worked in the fields, and spent very little time indoors. I disliked the classroom and in particular the library; the library did not have any windows, and I suffered from claustrophobia there. I needed to be able to see grass, trees, and sky. While the karate class would also be inside, the workout room was large, open, had a high ceiling and, best of all, it had large windows on one wall and a mirror on the opposite wall. I felt a lot more comfortable being inside in this environment.

The instructor welcomed me, asked me my name, explained that Tae Kwon Do is the Korean version of martial arts, and told me to address him as Mr. H.

"When entering the Dojang, which is Korean for gym" Mr. H said, "we always stop and bow to show respect for the art. Like this," he demonstrated. He turned and faced the open part of the room, stood tall, slapped his flat hands against the point where the legs and hip come together, and holding the upper body straight, bent forward at the waist into a bow, keeping his eyes forward, not down at the floor.

"Keep your head up. This allows you to remain aware of your surroundings and any surprise attack."

I imitated Mr. H.

"Very good. When class begins, the students are to bow to the instructor, thereby paying respect to him or her as well. At the end of class, we always bow to the instructor and bow when leaving the Dojang. Most people call this place a Dojo, but Dojo is Japanese. Tae Kwon Do is Korean, and the Korean word for gym is Dojang. You are to address all students by using the honorific Mr. or Ms. followed by their last name."

I was scared that I might fail, but I remembered my grandfather's teachings to always do my best and to put my heart and soul into every endeavor.

I made it to almost every class after work. Once I learned a technique, I would practice it at home. At the next class my instructor would correct my technique, stance, and balance. Mr. H ran the class as a drill instructor would in the military, which made sense since the instructor was a war veteran, having served in Vietnam. While there were a lot of physical demands, after a few classes, I began to notice that my shoulder, neck, back, and knees seemed stronger and seemed to be working better. I also noticed less pain. Each class began with a lot of yoga and stretching, as well as other warm-up exercises. The hour-long workouts also included pushups, sit-ups, and other physical exercises. I noticed my overall health and attitude improving. During my stretching routines, I also practiced the deep-breathing exercises I had learned in psychology class. My mind seemed to be clearer than it had been in a long time — maybe in forever. I had found a focus and was pursuing my goals. I had quit listening to all the voices in my head and had found myself, something the Mormons would not let one do. Being a Mormon meant sleeping, eating, and breathing Mormonism. I had never felt at peace like I did now. I was able to free up my mind and focus on what seemed to be my own path. In that alone, I felt peace in my heart and a quietness in my mind such as I had never felt before.

After I'd been in class for several weeks, Mr. H. entered the Dojang. He held some papers and had a grin on his face. He moved to the front of the classroom.

"Attention," he said.

All the students hurried to get into line and in unison bowed to Mr. H.

Mr. H held the papers in his hand and held them in the air above his shoulder.

"There is going to be a martial arts tournament in three weeks. I expect all of you to enter and participate in either sparring or katas or both. You have three weeks to get ready."

"Why do we have to compete?" asked a girl at the end of the line.

"It will give you a gauge of where you are in your training. It will put you up against others ranked at your same level."

The girl nodded.

"I am going to leave these fliers with the tournament details here by the door. Pick one up on your way out. I will also post one on the bulletin board, just in case you lose your copy. Okay, let's get started."

I felt awkward with my new moves. I didn't want to compete. I worked out as hard as or harder than the rest of the class and practiced techniques at home.

"Mr. H., would you mind showing me the technique on the heavy bag that you were showing us last class?" I asked.

Mr. H. was barely five feet six inches and weighed one hundred forty pounds, but he could really drill the heavy bag with a couple of different kicks, one in particular. Mr. H. was also older than forty and could still do the splits.

He showed me where to stand — about ten feet from the heavy bag. "Step through with your back leg, and bring your leg forward, through, and up, leading with your knee," he explained. "As you do this, turn your head to the left, rotating counterclockwise, elevate off the floor and spin around. As your body turns in the air, at about 180 degrees into the turn, extend your leg and strike with the heel of your foot. This is called a jump turn back kick, and it is the most powerful technique a human can deliver. The kick is very similar to a mule kick, but you have the ability to elevate and rotate your body."

One night after class, Mr. H. instructed us to put our sparring gear on. This included foam-padded gloves on each hand, padded covering for the feet, a groin cup for the males, and a mouthpiece.

"Leon, come on up," Mr. H. directed me into the invisible sparring ring, a ten-foot-by-ten-foot square. I had had some fights along the way in life, but never against someone of my teacher's skill. Even though Mr. H. was small in stature, he demonstrated tremendous power on the heavy bag. I was cautious as we moved around. All the fighting I had done before was usually when I was drunk or really angry. I had poor technique and was poorly prepared to fight a black belt. I made a huge error and moved into my instructor's leg range. Mr. H. delivered a back kick to my ribs, knocking the wind out of me and fracturing a couple of ribs. It would take me a couple of months to heal from this shot. At first I was angry with Mr. H. and questioned his ability to teach. Is this how he taught? Pick on a new student and break his ribs? From then on, I did not trust Mr. H.

I practiced as I was physically able to, working around my sore ribs. As my ribs were healing class after class, I showed up early so I could work on my techniques. Some were complex, complicated, and extra difficult for students with long arms and legs like I had. This was especially true for all the turn and jump-turn kicks.

One night a few weeks later, I showed up before class and worked on basic blocks, punches, and kicks. I looked at the clock and realized that there were only a few minutes left before class, so I went over to the heavy bag. I practiced the moves in slow motion, basically walking through each step keeping my feet on the floor. I was beginning to understand the balance required to develop the technique and the flow of movements. I began to pick up my speed, following my teacher's instruction. Mr. H. said if I could do it slowly and correctly, then I would be able to do it with speed and power. If one trains with rapid movements, then the technique will be off, and one will end up training with bad technique. Technique is the most important thing in achieving speed and power, he had explained. I brought my rear leg through, and as I turned my head, my supporting foot slid out from under me because of the dusty floor and my poor balance. My body continued to spin, and I caught myself falling to the floor and caught myself with my right hand and arm. I was in a great deal of pain.

"Are you all right?" a member of the spa came rushing over to where I'd fallen.

"No, I'm not all right," I said. "I think I've injured myself."

This was my second injury in Tae Kwon Do, and as I was also enrolled at U.T. Arlington, I got through the night and went into the clinic in the morning to see Dr. Garrett.

"Does this hurt?" the doctor asked at various points throughout the examination.

"Hell, yes, it hurts, Doc; that's why I came in."

"Let's get some x-rays."

I was directed to the x-ray room and climbed onto the table. The technician painfully placed my arm into various positions as he loaded film into the machine and scurried away to take the x-ray from behind a wall.

Back in the exam room, the doctor told me that I had two fractures at the elbow. The spinning and my weight behind the move I'd made in practice caused a fracture to the bone in two places at the socket of my right elbow.

"We need to put your lower and upper arm in a plaster cast. Here's a prescription for pain (more opioids); take it as needed. If you keep the elbow elevated above your heart, you will have less swelling and, therefore, less pain. If you let your elbow hang down, it'll swell, and you'll experience a lot more pain." I had just overcome an addiction to opioids. Now my doctor was suggesting I take more.

The work on the hotel had come to a close, and a lot of the workers, including me, were laid off. I went to the local unemployment office and filed for unemployment. I was granted unemployment compensation and was making it through my first semester at U.T. Arlington on the unemployment benefits. This allowed me to keep my savings intact for when I really needed it.

I called my father: "Dad, I am making it through this first semester okay, but I'm going to need you to repay the loan as you promised me. I am going to need that money for the next semester," I told him.

"Sorry," Dad said, "I don't have the money."

"You have stolen from me since I was nine years old. Now you have fabricated a lie to get some of my college money. You sold the two calves I had earned by working; you stole the jar of coins I had saved up when I was fourteen, and you have never ever kept a promise to me. Your word is simply bullshit, and you call yourself a fine Mormon? I'll be coming to visit in a couple of weeks. If you don't have the money to repay the loan, I'm going to beat the hell out of you, you got it?" I was livid.

I had enrolled in some of the toughest classes I had ever taken and would ever take. I was taking statistics, contract law, Spanish, and geology. Interestingly, my Spanish teacher was from Czechoslovakia and still spoke English with a heavy Czech accent. My other professors were very demanding, especially my statistics professor. My classes started at 9 a.m. and lasted until 1 p.m. Statistics class was two nights a week at seven, and one night each week the class lasted for two hours, as a statistics graduate student would come to class to help us undergraduates after the professor left. I had a cast on my right arm, my dominant arm, and was now forced to make my left arm dominant. I began using my left hand to make notes. At best, my notes were just above the level of a scribble.

Now, after more than thirty years, I was finally using my naturally dominant arm and hand. My first statistics and probabilities test came up when I was still in a cast. I thought I knew the material but scored a thirty-six out of 100. I was devastated but realized that the opioids I was taking for pain were inhibiting my ability to think clearly. My arm was getting better, but it swelled up, hurt, and throbbed, and I took the pain meds. As usual, I was determined and stayed with the class, because if I dropped out, I would get a score of withdrawal with an F. This was a required class for my major, which I had now determined would be psychology. So, I buckled down and doubled up on my studies in statistics. I also struggled with my other classes, but I was at least passing them. Soon my second test in statistics came up. I spent a lot of time studying and preparing for this test; however, I still had a lot of pain in my arm, and I was still taking the pain meds. I scored a forty-seven out of 100. It was not quite as bad as it sounded because the tests were extremely difficult, and the professor graded on a curve. Nevertheless, I was still failing after two tests. I was beside myself and approached my statistics professor in the hall before class. I explained what I had been going through and that I felt like I really did know the material. I asked him if he'd ever had a student recover from test scores as bad as mine and still pass the course.

"Nope," the professor said, bursting my bubble of hope.

"I really need this class. Do you have any suggestions?" I tried again.

"You can discuss your situation with my assistant, the grad student. Maybe he'll have some suggestions." The professor sounded doubtful.

I thanked him. My head was spinning as I found the assistant's office the next day. As I entered the office, I could see the silhouette of the assistant against the backdrop of the wall of windows. The walls to the right and left were completely filled with bookshelves. The young man behind the desk looked small in this overcrowded room.

"Do you have a few minutes? I would like to discuss my options with you," I said.

"Sure. Come on in and have a seat," he offered.

I took a seat in the one empty chair in front of the desk. The other chair was piled with books and papers.

I explained my dilemma.

"Go over to the bookstore and purchase Schaum's Outline on Statistics and Probabilities. Then go over to the library and check out a book or two on elementary statistics and probabilities. Work whatever problems you can as far as you can and bring them to me, and I will show you how to finish the problems," he said.

The assistant's advice seemed sound, and I went with it. I had no idea if I could really do what was required, but I knew that if I didn't run the race and finish it, I would never win, and I needed this class. I got the books the assistant suggested I get. Since I was not attending Tae Kwon Do Classes, I studied statistics every night. I sat down on the floor and placed my reference books around me, working on as many problems as I could. I solicited the assistance of the professor's assistant a few times, and he helped me as he said he would. As the final exam was coming up, I had my cast removed, and my arm had greatly improved. There was some pain, so I went back to the doctor. Dr. Garrett took my right wrist and put his other hand on my elbow and performed a quick technique, popping my elbow. The pain went from a level eight to maybe a level two, and I was now able to straighten out my arm.

I returned home after class one afternoon and was surprised to find a check from my father. He had finally followed through, but only after I'd threatened him.

I showed up for the final exam in statistics. I had read and worked problems from the six books I had checked out of the Library and purchased from the bookstore. I had taken the problems I'd worked on to the professor's assistant and worked through the problems I had missed. I was as prepared as I could possibly be. The classroom seemed too large for the number of students who would be testing. The class had started in the fall with about sixty students, but only ten of us showed up for the final exam. That left a lot of space in the classroom. I had prepared for the final exam by studying and by doing a lot of meditation. This was an open-book test, so I gathered three desks around me so I could have all my reference books and study books nearby, and I had my battery-operated statistical calculator with me as well. The final exam consisted of ten statistical problems. About three hours later the professor collected everyone's answer sheets. The test had taken more than three hours to work on only ten problems.

By the following morning, the tests had been graded, and results were posted in the hallway outside the classroom. The answer sheets were available to be returned to us students if we picked them up at the professor's office. Hoping I had passed the class, I approached the score sheet on the wall. I was already trying to figure out what I would need to do if I failed this required class. I needn't have worried. My score was the second highest in class. The only student scoring higher than I did was a student who had taken the same class three years earlier and had come back only for a refresher. I got an A- on the final exam and effectively earned a C for the semester, passing the class! Only six of the ten who sat for the final exam passed! I felt like I was Superman; my confidence was soaring beyond my wildest dreams. I had passed what might be the most difficult freshman-level university class in existence, and I ended up doing it the hard way. Additionally, most of the time I was under the influence of opioids, and I had to come back from two badly failed tests. I had beaten the addiction this time. My focus and meditation took me over the top, and I conquered something I never thought I would ever be able to conquer.

After my arm healed sufficiently, I returned to practicing Tae Kwon Do a little here and there. I began attending classes again. Mr. H. brought in a tournament flier. The tournament, Kurban's annual Pro-Am Karate Tournament, was to be held in Fort Worth and would be hosted by a Master Kurban, who ran a school in Arlington called the "American Black Belt Academy."

I was still a white belt. Mr. H seldom administered belt tests, but I had been training for a few months for this tournament. I showed up on Saturday morning, paid my entry fee, and prepared for my first-ever tournament match. I could street fight, but this contest had rules, required discipline, a referee, and it had a time limit.

The tournament was held in Fort Worth. I entered the gym and stood in line for the registration table.

"Name," the registration clerk asked.

"Leon Mecham."

"You will be competing in ring 13," she said. I'd always felt that thirteen was my lucky number. That had been the number I wore on my basketball jersey in high school.

The aide pointed me to a set of double doors and directed me to ring 13 on the far side of the room.

"Where can I change into my gi?" I asked.

"The locker rooms are on the far side of the gym," she said. "There is a sign over the entrance to each."

I smiled at the girl and turned to go through the doors. Inside the gym, I saw two walls of pull-out wooden bleachers. On the open floor, tape was placed to identify fourteen separate ten-foot-by-ten-foot rings. Inside each ring, at the center, were two 24-inch tape lines, one on each side of the ring. This is where the competitors would stand until the ring judge gave the command to start the fight, and it is where they would return each time the judge called break.

At the end of the room near the double doors I'd come through were four white folding tables. My eyes widened as I saw what looked like hundreds of trophies lined up. There were small third-place trophies, medium-sized second-place trophies, and tall first-place trophies that were topped with a figure that had its leg extended and its arms in a protective pose, hands in fists. There were trophies with both male and female figures throwing martial arts kicks.

I went into the locker room, found an empty locker, changed into my gi, and placed the combination lock onto the door of my locker.

I found a quiet place to sit and meditate a few minutes before the tournament began.

There was a formal bow in to start off the tournament. Everyone present — judges, assistants, competitors, and those who came to watch the tournament — all stood and said the Pledge of Allegiance to the flag of the United States. Master Kurban had appointed the head ring judge to go over the rules of the tournament.

Everyone went to their assigned rings. The judge at ring 13 reviewed the list of competitors and identified the order in which competitors would spar.

I had decided not to compete in the katas and would be only sparring.

I watched the first two competitors step into the ring. I watched closely so I would do it correctly when it was my turn.

Before each competitor stepped into the ring, he bowed toward the ring. He then walked to the 24-inch line indicated by the judge. Once both competitors were standing at their line, an assistant ring judge tied a red ribbon to the back of the belt of one competitor. This allowed the judges to know who had scored a point.

Once the fighters were in their positions, they were instructed to bow to the judges.

Both bowed toward the judges.

"Bow to each other," the judge instructed.

Each bowed to his opponent.

"Fighters ready?" the judge asked.

Both nodded to the judge.

"Fight," the judge said as he dropped his right arm and hand in a hatchet-like movement.

I watched as the competitors began. They raised their hands up, prepared to block or throw punches, and began to bob and shuffle their feet. For the first few seconds, this is all they did as each sized up his opponent. I began to wonder if this was all they were going to do. Suddenly, one competitor moved in and threw a right jab followed by a left ridge hand strike to the side of his opponent's head. The opponent dodged the right and blocked the left, then threw his own punch followed by a kick to the abdominal area.

"Break," the judge called.

Both competitors returned to their designated lines. The judge looked at the other two judges in the ring. They each held up the red end of the red and white stick the judges used to identify which opponent they saw score.

"Two points red. Fight."

The competitors started again. This continued until the two-minute sparring round ended. It ended when a timer seated at the table at the head of the ring threw a bean bag into the ring.

I was to compete next.

I bowed before entering the ring and walked to the indicated line. I bowed to the judges and to my opponent.

Then the ref, his arm raised, asked, "Fighters ready?" My opponent and I nodded to the judge, who dropped his hand to waist level and said, "Fight!" My first match began.

I stepped in and to the right slightly. My opponent turned to the left, but as he did so, he opened up his rib cage. I drove my right hand forward, throwing a reverse punch toward my opponent's ribs. The only problem was that the opponent moved more than I had anticipated he would, and I missed my target, locking out my right elbow, the one that had just healed. I grabbed my right elbow. "Break," shouted the ref as he stepped in. He looked toward the other two judges, and they both held their right hands to their eyebrows, palms toward the floor. This indicated they had not seen any points earned.

"No point. Are you all right?" asked the ref.

I rubbed my elbow and returned to my line, ready to go again and moved into my fighting stance.

"Ready, fight!" yelled the ref, and we started again.

I knew if I continued to use my right arm, I would re-injure it, and it would take weeks to heal again.

I watched my opponent. When I saw an opening, without even thinking about it, I stepped in and, using only one-quarter power, kicked my opponent in the groin.

"Break," said the ref, quieter this time.

"Two points, white." The one without the red flag was considered white. I did not have the flag.

The match went on like this for two minutes, and I was declared the winner. As standard procedure, we fighters bowed to the ref before leaving the ring. I didn't know that Mr. H. had watched the event. He stepped up to me as I exited the ring.

"Leon, you injured your elbow, didn't you?" he asked.

"I'm all right," I lied.

"No, you are not, you need to bow out of this tournament," Mr. H. demanded.

"I can win this thing," I insisted.

"You are going to bow out so you don't hurt yourself more. If you continue, it may take several weeks for your elbow to heal, or you could permanently injure yourself."

I already knew this, but I had come to compete and did not want to quit. I had never been a quitter. "Okay, Mr. H., how do I do that?"

Mr. H spoked with the ring judge. The judge called me back into the ring and had me formally bow out of the tournament. Because I was interested in the tournament, I stayed and watched the black belts compete.

I was frustrated, but I knew that bowing out was the smart thing to do. I didn't want to re-injure my elbow. I enjoyed competing. Even though I'd had to bow out, I felt I had done well. I began getting my mind ready for the next opportunity. I had learned a few things watching the black belts, and I had a renewed desire to learn and compete.

I participated more in sparring in class. I hated sparring with my teacher but felt good sparring with others. I was usually larger than my classmates, except for Joe. Joe was approximately the same height and weight as I was. I trained more frequently, worked harder, and improved significantly.

A few months after the tournament, the U.S. Open Karate championship was scheduled to come to the Dallas area.

I not only trained, but I also continued my studies.

The first semester at U.T. Arlington had taught me some valuable lessons. The expense to take a university class per credit hour was about three times what it cost at the junior college I had attended. Second, the degree of difficulty for passing a class was at least three times greater. And last, the university campus was about ten times the size of the campus at the junior college. It was much easier to park and get to the classrooms at the junior college.

The next spring, I re-enrolled at the junior college. I could take more hours, have less expense, and the basic required courses were much easier than the university courses. I completed all the required freshman- and sophomore-level courses for my degree. I also took some electives.

I finally earned my two-year associate's degree and got my certificate of graduation. I had also excelled in psychology studies; Dr. Mount, the head of the psychology department named me an honor student. I graduated from Mountain View Junior College with honors. Not only did I excel in my course studies, but also a young, tall brunette had attracted my attention. She was fourteen years younger than I, and I thought she was one of the most beautiful women I had ever seen. She was the pursuer, and I played along for a while, enjoying my new girlfriend. She even occasionally attended Tae Kwon Do class with me.

I dated her throughout the summer and worked to make a little extra money. Fall came; I enrolled again at the university and continued preparing for the U.S. Open. To prepare for the level of difficulty and expense at the university, I also applied for the work-study program. I was accepted and assigned an office on the fourth floor of the biology/psychology building across and down a couple of doors from the head of the psychology department. I enrolled in geology, psychology, and property law. I was doing fairly well, except the class I was taking was "abnormal psych," and I began having nightmares again similar to those I had experienced as an adolescent. I had not experienced these kinds of bloody nightmares in many years, so I asked my professor for a private meeting. I divulged to my professor what was going on with the nightmares. She seemed genuinely concerned and said she would get back to me. She saw me at the next class and briefly met with me to suggest I call the Tarrant County Mental Health organization. I began attending anger-management group sessions a few days after. After a few weeks, I felt I had worked through that, and I stopped attending the sessions. There were some seriously angry people there, and I felt out of place. Besides, the sessions took time out of my education in Tae Kwon Do and kept me away from my studies. I didn't feel that I was benefiting from my time spent there. On top of all that, the U.S. Open Karate Championship was coming up. I was eager to participate, as I had had only one match at the previous tournament before bowing out.

The big competition day finally arrived. The U.S. Open was being held at Eastfield Junior College in Garland. I paid my entry fee and got ready for my first match. The setup was similar to the one I'd seen before. I easily won my first match and got ready for my second match. My second opponent was the same build and height as I was, maybe a little stockier; he was also about ten years younger than I. My opponent was also better prepared and won the match.

Back home, Mr. H. asked me how I did at the tournament.

"Not worth a damn," I told him. "My ribs hurt, and I lost in the second round. He must have nailed me in my left ribs with a reverse punch at least four times."

"Remember to keep your left elbow in tight, and that won't happen," Mr. H. advised.

"I like participating in tournaments," I told him, "but I don't want another ass whipping like that again!"

Mr. H. gave me a serious look and said, "Before the next tournament comes up, I want you to do 5,000 of these, 5,000 of these, and 5,000 of these," demonstrating an upper block, a reverse punch, and a back kick.

"Okay, I get the message, more repetitions," I conceded. It would be a few months before I would participate in another tournament. I had participated as a yellow belt at the U.S. Open and would be participating as a blue belt at the next tournament. At my age, I was on the cusp of my age division. Some tournaments had divisions of age thirty-two and older; some had the bracket set at age thirty-five and older. I would be thirty-four years old at the state championship. Up until then I had been competing in the open age group, heavyweight division. At the next tournament I would compete at the executive, or old man's, level.

I vowed to be better prepared for this tournament. After all, I did not want another ass whipping like I got at the U.S. Open. I went to tournaments because I wasn't sure Mr. H. was teaching the good stuff. I also went to tournaments to see how I measured up against others of the same age, belt, and weight class. I never trusted Mr. H. after he kicked me in the ribs. I felt that a teacher was supposed to teach, not injure his students.

My university studies were going well. I got into a groove. I gained a lot of confidence after passing statistics, especially because of how it happened. I met with Dr. Cain, the head of the psychology department, to get my first job assignment under the work-study program.

"Leon, here are six boxes of Texas State Prison reports," said Dr. Cain as he led me to a file storage room. "I believe there are about 1,500 reports in total. I need you to read them, build a filing system, and file them in that upright four-drawer file cabinet. Feel free to come to my office anytime and ask me any questions you have regarding these reports."

"Yes, sir," I responded.

I was taking only four classes, but they were very difficult classes, and I had never been a particularly good student. And now my Tae Kwon Do training was harder than ever. But yoga and Tae Kwon Do helped me keep in shape and gave me some relief, as I had always enjoyed physical and strenuous exercises and tasks. This gave me a way to work hard physically and helped to keep my mind clear, which would benefit me in working for Dr. Cain and helping him with prison research, for which he was internationally renowned.

I had also passed another belt test and had been awarded my blue belt. Mr. H. owned a small company and had been getting really busy. Just before class one night, Mr. H. called the health spa where the Tae Kwon Do classes were held and asked for me.

"Leon, can you take class tonight?" he asked.

"Yes sir, no problem," I agreed to help.

I began teaching Tae Kwon Do as Mr. H.'s assistant. I would go to class an hour early and get my workout in because when I taught class, I was not able to get as much work in for myself. This worked out great, especially when I showed up an hour early and then Mr. H. would come to class and teach. Those nights, I got in a two-hour workout in. I would lose as much as ten pounds in a two-hour work-out, due to water loss. My flexibility was better than it had been since I was a baby. My shoulder, knee, and back pain were almost gone. The knee pain wasn't completely gone because there were still bone fragments under and on the right side of the right kneecap, which my high school football coach had shattered when he tackled me. To help stabilize my knee joints, I wore steel-hinged knee braces when I sparred.

Fall came and the 20th Annual Texas State Karate Championships were going to be held in Fort Worth at the Tarrant County Convention Center. I felt ready.

I went to the convention center on a Saturday. At registration, I learned that I would participate in a division of age thirty-two and older. I was almost thirty-five, so I was easily over the age required to compete in that division. My objective was to match myself up with others of the same age, belt, and weight. In this division there was no weight requirement, so I competed with light- and middle-weight contestants as well as heavyweights. I was so prepared and so ready, I walked through the competition smoothly, as if I had been fighting only white belts. I had hardly broken a sweat. I told my girlfriend, who'd come with me to the tournament, that I wanted to stop by Mr. H.'s house on the way home.

"Hey, Leon," he greeted us. "How are you doing? Come on in. So, how did you do at the tournament?"

I wanted to remain humble and did not want to boast. "They gave me a trophy for showing up," I said.

"Well, go get it; I want to see it," Mr. H. insisted.

I went out and got the trophy, and as I carried it inside, Mr. H's eyes widened, and a grin spread across his face.

I had won trophies for different things but had never won anything like this. The trophy was about eighteen inches tall and made of bronze. It held a detailed statuette of a karate fighter in his gi. It read, "1st Place Executive Division 20th Annual Texas State Karate Championships." I had never been so proud of my success.

"Be sure to bring that trophy to class Tuesday night," Mr. H. said.

That week, I arrived at class early, as usual. I placed the trophy behind some equipment in a corner so no one would see it before I showed the class. After Mr. H. called the class to order and everyone had bowed in, Mr. H. said, "Leon, do you have something to share with the class?"

"Yes, sir." I walked over to where I had placed the trophy.

As the trophy came into view, I could hear gasps from the other students. I carried it back to the front of the class. My face was lit up by the twinkle in my eyes and the huge grin on my face. The other students gathered around to admire my trophy.

Before long, I took another belt exam and easily made first-degree red belt, then a few months later, I made second-degree red belt, and then third-degree red belt.

By now I was very comfortable sparring with anyone. I had even visited a few other schools and sparred with other students. Some of my friends said they saw a new swagger in my gait. I was not aware of any difference, but I was attuned to the change in my level of confidence. I had always tried to avoid confrontations, but now, if someone wanted to get it on, I felt I was more prepared to defend myself.

On the education front, I kept my nose in my schoolbooks and continued to get passing grades. I even made the dean's honor roll a time or two; I was closing in on my bachelor's degree. I had tried to break it off with my girlfriend, but she insisted that I was the man for her. She had listened to what I wanted and said she wanted the same things. She was putting in much more effort than I was to keep the relationship going, so I thought that if she wanted it that badly, then maybe we should get married. It had been more than three years since my second divorce, and I had gotten over that relationship a long time ago.

I saw my boys somewhat infrequently but enough to keep asking them the same two questions: where are you going to college and what are you going to study? I'd get them in the summer for a week or so; I'd bring them to my place and take them to Tae Kwon Do class, where I'd teach them some techniques.

Spring of 1985 came, and I needed two more classes to graduate in addition to the ones I had committed to take, but the classes I needed were not on either the spring or summer schedules. I went to the registrar's office and explained to the counselor my dilemma. The advisor told me to visit with the two professors who taught the individual classes and ask if they would be willing to help. After discussing my situation with the professors, each allowed me to study on my own and be periodically tested. I passed both classes easily and received my bachelor's degree in the Summer of 1985. I was now a university graduate and holder of the first-place trophy in my division at the 20th annual Texas State Karate Championships.

In three years, I had met and far exceeded my goals and objectives in learning self-defense. Not only had I become proficient, I was able to kick some butt, and I could do it quickly.

I graduated from college and married my third wife. Now I had to go to work as I was broke; I had spent all the money I had earned plus my savings, and had had to borrow $10,000 to finish my bachelor's degree.

I was lost and a little tired. I had been so focused on two things for the last three and a half years that I had not thought of much of anything else. I had put my heart and soul into my studies and Tae Kwon Do, far exceeding my own expectations. I had to find and make new goals.

Another tournament was coming up, and I wanted to compete one more time. This was the Sun Belt Open, at the time the largest karate tournament in Texas. It was being held at Loos Field Stadium in North Dallas.

I showed up and paid my entry fee. I had established a tournament routine: first, check in at or before 8 a.m., then change clothes and meditate. After beating my competitor, I would find the ring for my next match, meditate again, beat my competitor, and so on. Meditation had become a vital part of my martial arts routine. On this day, I won my matches leading up to the final match. I was looking for a tournament official to verify the ring I was to compete in next. I was informed that I would have to come back the next day, Sunday, to compete for the finals. This was unusual. Tournaments typically lasted one day. The only problem was that I had other plans for Sunday.

"I'm sorry, but I'm not coming tomorrow," I advised the official.

"Why? It's the finals; don't you want to compete for first place?" The official was confused.

"Look, I didn't know I would be required to compete tomorrow. I made other plans. I'll fight another fight today if you have someone for me to fight." I didn't give a rat's ass about the large plastic trophies they were giving out. I came for the competition.

"Have a seat over there," the official said, pointing to the bleachers. "We'll be back in a few minutes." The official walked over to a group of officials at the head table and began to confer.

I waited for a few minutes until the officials started my way. They brought another person with them, an African American male about two or three inches taller than I and about forty pounds heavier. On the back of my opponent's karate gi was the man's nickname, The Devil. I had refused to fight the Devil on Sunday, not that I cared at all about what day it was; I was too busy being an asshole. In those days, I said what I wanted to say and didn't care who I said it to. I might have been labeled as "one who does not play well with others."

When the ring cleared and the judges made arrangements for the competition, I waited patiently. When the officials were ready, I stepped into the ring and waited to be directed to my official starting place. The ring judge stepped up. He looked at each of us and asked if we were ready. We both acknowledged that we were. The judge stepped between us, held his hand up, and as he dropped his right hand he said, "Fight." I had set up with my right side in front. As the judge dropped his hand, I began my first move. I brought my back (left) leg, emphasizing my forward momentum and elevating myself off the floor. As I elevated, I turned my head to the right, setting my body into a clockwise spin with my arms and legs tight to my body. As I rotated about 270 degrees, I extended my right heel as quickly as I could into the target. I made contact with the Devil's ribs and kicked him out of the ring. Break, the refs commanded. The Devil told the ref that he had tripped and fallen out of the ring. The ref held his flag down and said no points. He then set us in position, raised his hand again, and said "Fight." This time I set up, left side in front and stepped quickly to my right. As the Devil turned his body to the right, I moved to the left and in tight. I delivered a right punch to his chin with control as we were not allowed to make full contact with our opponent's face. I had stopped the punch a couple of inches short. Again, the ref called a break. Again he held the flag low and announced, "no points." I looked at the judge and shrugged my shoulders to ask what the hell was going on, and he glared back. The next time the ref said "Fight," the Devil extended his right foot as though he were executing a front kick. There were only two problems with this. First, the Devil might have been taller and heavier, but he was also a lot slower. I saw the kick coming from last week and easily executed a block. Second, I didn't block the kick as it was about three feet away from connecting with any part of my body. Break! The ring judge held up his flag and announced two points for the Devil. Same thing happened when we fought again. The Devil delivered a slow kick, and it stopped short of making contact with me. The ring judge was black, as was my opponent. I wasn't sure if I was being discriminated against or if I was just being punished because of my poor attitude that day.

After I had refused to abide by the rules, there was no way the officials were going to give me the first-place trophy. That was okay with me, as my opponent and I both knew who won the match. I was comfortable taking the second-place trophy.

Now on to make some money and start a new life for my beautiful wife and me! I thought my wife was absolutely beautiful, and I adored her.

My trophy for winning the Texas State
Karate Championship in 1984.

With my first-degree black belt,
presented to me on Sept. 17, 2022.

CHAPTER 7

Construction, Third Marriage, and General Contracting

For years, I had been in school, working hard to earn my bachelor's degree and learning the art of self-defense. Between school and my ex-family, my relationship with my boys had stalled. The boys were able to come to my third wedding, as did so many other people who were prominent in my life. Professor James made it, and so had quite a few others. The wedding had escalated and evolved into a graduation party, as well.

Before the wedding, James congratulated me. I thanked him for coming, and we talked a bit about what he'd been up to.

"The wife and I are doing well," he said. "We just got back from a trip to Europe."

"How was the trip?" I asked.

"It was great, relaxing, and informative. Sam couldn't quit smiling."

"Sounds like a lot of fun."

Then, looking at my hand, James asked, "Where is your graduation ring?"

I told him that a graduation ring was not in my budget.

"How much are they?" Professor James asked.

"They're about $300 for the ones with 10-karat gold settings," I said. I had been by the student center and bookstore and had seen the rings but figured I had other, more important things on which to spend my money, like my education and food.

"Here," James said, handing over cash. "Sam and I want you to have a graduation ring."

"That's very generous of you, but I couldn't accept that," I argued.

"The heck you can't," James said. "Here is $300, and I don't want to hear any reasons why you can't accept it. Consider it a wedding gift, if you must."

I nearly fainted when I considered the generosity of Professor James and his wife, Samantha. They'd paid for the wedding cake and the groom's cake, and now a graduation ring. The groom's cake was decorated in UTA colors to celebrate all the hard work and dedication I had put into my education.

I was broke, so I did what I knew how to do. I began visiting construction sites looking for a job as a carpenter. I figured I would work at construction and get a few dollars in my pocket until I was able to get some direction in my possible new career. I wasn't sure where I was headed in my career, so a carpentry job would suffice for now. I planned to visit a site I had been referred to, a large construction job where a church was being built. It just so happened the church was a Mormon church in Duncanville.

I was driving a 1964 Chevy C-30 panel truck, as I had sold my newer pickup years before to pay for tuition and books. The twenty-year-old, six-cylinder motor was leaking oil badly and needed to be freshened up and rebuilt. I remembered hearing that Mr. H could do mechanical work, so at Tae Kwon Do class, I asked him about it, telling him I believed my truck needed a new motor.

"I'm sorry to hear that," he said. "I understand you are a carpenter. Are you any good?" he countered.

"I'm the best," I told him.

"My house just happens to need some carpentry work. When you get a chance, come by and I'll show you the damage to the house. Maybe we can work something out."

I stopped by Mr. H.'s house a couple of days later and saw that the wood siding around the perimeter of the house had been rotting due to weather, lack of paint, and vegetation around the foundation.

"I can take the siding off and put up new siding if you will rebuild the motor in my truck," I said, "I will pay for the materials for your house, and you pay for the parts needed for the truck. The only problem is that I need a vehicle to get to work and back."

"I'll order the parts for your truck," Mr. H said. "In the meantime, while I am getting the parts, you can replace the wood siding on my house."

"Works for me," I agree. "My boys are coming up next week; I'll get them to help me."

I purchased the material for Mr. H.'s house, and Mr. H. ordered the parts for my truck. My sons came up to visit, and I had them help take the old siding off and install the new siding. I also took them to Tae Kwon Do in the evenings.

We completed the siding, and I asked Mr. H about the status of my truck parts. He said he had some of the parts.

"I can start on the motor this weekend," he said. "It should go quickly. You can drive Old Red until I get your motor installed." Old Red was Mr. H.'s older Ford F-100 he had restored. He called it Old Red as he had painted it fire engine red.

I took my truck to Mr. H. 's shop, and we met and swapped keys and trucks.

"Be sure to check the oil in Red frequently," Mr. H advised. "Even though I rebuilt the motor, it's an old truck and needs a watchful eye."

I had completed my part of the agreement, but Mr. H. was not progressing with repairs as I had expected. He seemed to have one excuse after another.

After about a week, I checked in again. "Mr. H., how are the repairs coming along? Did you get those parts in?"

"The motor rebuild company sent me a bad short block. I just got a replacement in," he said. "I've taken the heads in to get the valves checked along with the valve springs, etc."

"It's been more than a week and approaching two weeks," I said. "I was expecting it to be done based on what you told me."

"Well, it's a damn Chevrolet, and nothing seems to be coming together," he said.

"Mr. H., if you spent as much time working on that damn Chevrolet as you do dreaming up excuses, you would have already been done with it."

Mr. H's eyes narrowed, and his face turned bright red. Anger radiated off him like a heater.

"All right," Mr. H growled. "You and me… at the dojang… Tuesday night!" he challenged, jabbing a finger in my face.

I was confused by Mr. H's violent reaction. A fight wouldn't resolve the problem. I had done the repairs to Mr. H.'s house, and Mr. H. had not repaired my truck.

I knew that Mr. H. had not been putting in his best effort to get my truck done. I was tired of all the excuses, so I spoke my mind. The only problem I had was that I now placed myself in a position of having to make a huge decision: fight my teacher or quit Tae Kwon Do. But I had put too much effort into my training to just quit, so I came up with a simple game plan. It was the same plan I had used throughout the five tournaments in which I had competed. The first rule was don't hurt myself. The second rule was don't let the other guy hurt me. And the final rule was to make every effort to win, within the rules.

Tuesday night came. I was more nervous than I had been in a long time. I had watched my teacher spar with numerous individuals and felt that I would be able to anticipate most of Mr. H's moves. I was concerned about moves I had not seen and those I might possibly miss.

I was on edge. I didn't know when we were going to spar. I wanted to get it over with. Mr. H. bowed in class, as usual. He took the class through various techniques and reviewed one of the katas.

Looking directly at me, Mr. H. said, "Get your gear on." The teaching part of the class had ended, and there were a few minutes left.

"I have my knee braces on, and I have what I need, except for my mouthpiece," I said as I placed my mouthpiece in, stood up, and took my position in the sparring area.

Mr. H. did pretty much what I expected but somehow Mr. H was able to position himself in tight with me. Now my teacher was close enough to punch me in the body or the head and close enough to execute a variety of kicks to my body or head.

I blocked all the punches Mr. H threw at me, most of which were directed to my head. I saw an opening but chose to not try to hit or kick Mr. H. I had no desire to embarrass my teacher, even if I could make contact. Mr. H. had helped me. If not for Mr. H., I might never have learned Tae Kwon Do.

Almost four years before, when I had been accepted into the university, I had approached Mr. H. I explained that I'd be going to school full time and that I wouldn't have time to work, that I might need to borrow money to finish my education. "This is to let you know that I won't have funds to pay monthly dues for Tae Kwon Do lessons," I told him.

"Leon, you see that heavy bag over there?" Mr. H. had pointed across the room.

"Yes, sir."

"If I leave it there all the time, it will get damaged. In this setting with all the people coming into the spa, someone will kick it with their shoes on, and the canvas cover is susceptible to getting torn. To pay for lessons, I want you to take that bag down after every class, take it home with you, and bring it back with you to the next class."

"No problem. I would love to take care of the bag," I had promised, keeping in mind that the workout area was on the fourth floor of the old J.C. Penney building, and the elevator worked only some of the time. This meant that I had to carry the bag down four flights of stairs and rehang it before every class. Thank God, the bag weighed only about eighty pounds. This was not only a strength exercise, but also an exercise in hand-eye coordination, because I had to get the loop and chain connected when I hung the bag back up. And besides carrying the bag up and down stairs, I had to get it out the back door and across the parking lot, depending on how close I could park. My legs, knees, and back were a lot stronger after I did this a few dozen times.

Despite my lack of trust in my teacher, I greatly respected Mr. H for being so dedicated to the sport that he allowed me to work out my tuition for classes. I was not in any way interested in hurting my teacher nor embarrassing him. Attempting to hit or kick Mr. H in this unscheduled match was not an option for me.

After a few minutes of sparring, Mr. H. had not delivered a punch or kick that had made contact with me. He had become frustrated and set up for an elevated side kick. I saw it coming and prepared my body to receive the blow. As Mr. H. began the move, I stepped to my left. Mr. H. made an effort to make a last-second adjustment, and in the process, his feet slipped out from under him, and he landed on his right hip and right elbow on the hard tile floor. It was all I could do to keep from laughing, but I held my composure. Mr. H. had hurt himself. We sparred another minute or two when he announced that we'd sparred enough for the night.

Mr. H. did eventually finish the work on my truck, and we maintained our relationship.

Life was rolling along. I had been asking around about work and had been given some information about a new building under construction in Duncanville. I drove around and found the building site and introduced myself to the construction foreman.

"What kind of work are you looking for?" the foreman asked.

"I am a framing carpenter," I replied. I noticed that the slab had been poured, and the 12-inch-by-12-inch-by-16-inch concrete block walls had been erected. Both the exterior and interior walls were of the same construction; the exterior would get a brick finish later. The interior would eventually get painted or get a drywall finish.

"Yes, we need some framing carpenters; when can you start?" The foreman asked.

"As soon as you are ready for me. What day and time do you want me here?" I was very accommodating.

The foreman told me to be on the job at 7 the next morning.

The next morning, a light rain fell as I was driving to work. A couple of blocks from the construction site, I saw a man walking along the side of the road. I briefly made eye contact with him and, inexplicably, got a bad vibe. I arrived at the construction site and checked in with the superintendent.

"Let's wait an hour or so and see if it's going to quit raining," he advised.

"I'll be in my truck over there, reading, if you need me," I replied, pointing to my old panel truck. I'd enrolled in a post graduate class that required a lot of reading, and I had brought along one of my books for just such an occasion.

I was reading about Chuck Yeager, the first person to break the sound barrier, when I was startled by someone jerking open the passenger door.

"What are you doing?" I demanded.

I recognized the man I'd passed who'd been walking along the road in the rain. "I came over to see what you're doing," he said.

"I'm busy preparing for my class. If you need to get out of the rain, go over to the job shack." I directed the wet man elsewhere.

He closed the door to my truck and left. I was unsettled by this incident, as it was extremely rude for him to open the door to my vehicle as if he were planning to enter it without being invited to do so. I continued to read, and after about an hour had passed, it was still raining, and the foreman announced that we'd shut down for the day. I headed for home. The next day I was assigned two young men to assist me in installing the ceiling joists, a few rafters, and lots of blocking and bracing.

My crew and I worked diligently all morning and then took lunch. I came back to my work area after lunch, where I again encountered the young man from the day before. He had unplugged my Rockwall 7-¼ -inch circular saw and was walking away with it. I was sure that this young man had been told the rules about company tools and where to find them.

"Hey, that's my saw!" I grabbed the saw from the young man. "This is my personal saw. If you need a saw, then go to that semi-trailer and get one. The company will provide one for you."

The young man shrugged his shoulders and walked off empty-handed. All went well the rest of the day, as my crew and I were cutting and nailing joists, stiff backs, and installing blocking. We finished one area and moved sawhorses, tools, and stocked up on lumber for the next area.

The next day after our lunch break, I returned to my work area and found this same young man carrying away my American brand wooden 4-foot level. There are a lot of things a man can do and get away with, but one should never, ever mess with a carpenter's level.

I grabbed my wood level; I was pissed. As I grabbed it with my left hand, I hit the young man on the left side of his face with my open right hand, delivering a "bitch slap," reminiscent of how my mother would slap me.

"I told you yesterday that if you needed a tool, to go to the job shack and get what you need," I told him. "These are my personal tools, not company tools! If you mess with me one more time, I will hurt you!" This was my final warning.

The young man walked off. I was six feet, four inches tall and now weighed about 215 pounds. I was flexible and extremely quick for a large-framed man, and more powerful than one would suspect. In preparing for tournaments, I was known to do 100-200 pushups a day on my knuckles, which made the push-ups about four inches longer than they would be if done using one's palms. I would also do 200-300 karate crunches a day, an abdominal exercise whereby one raises the head doing a sit-up and simultaneously pulls the knees to the chest. This young man was screwing with one bad son of a bitch who was not in a very good mood.

About an hour later, the young man returned to my work area. I was at the sawhorses cutting 2x8s to length. As the young man walked into the room where I was working, he yelled, "Now you big son a bitch, we are even!" He had gone to the lumber pile and selected a 2x4 about the length of a baseball bat and had driven nails through the end in different directions, creating a deadly weapon. He had taken a straight claw hammer and used the straight claws to whittle a handle into the 2x4. He swung the 2x4 over his right shoulder. This man was going to kill me, I thought. I knew I had to act instantly; there were no other doors except the one the young man came through. I was wearing my carpenter's leather tool belt that had a tape measure, a square, hammer, and lots of nails, adding about ten to fifteen pounds to my weight. There was an eight- to ten-foot distance between the man and me.

As the man began his swing, I took two quick steps and elevated by bringing my back leg through and my left knee upward. As I moved forward and upward, I turned my head to the right, shoulders following, putting myself into a clockwise spin. About 180 degrees into the spin, I extended my right leg, leading with my right heel. I intended to drive my heel deep into my attacker. I had closed the distance in midair and made contact with the young man's rib cage, breaking his ribs. The force of the kick propelled the young man backward into a concrete block wall. There was so much force in the kick that the young man bounced off the wall and back to me, landing me on two feet in a perfectly balanced position after striking. I turned my body to the right, effectively coiling and preparing for my next defensive move. As the young man came at me, falling and stumbling, I uncoiled by quickly twisting my upper body counter-clockwise. My right forearm and elbow made contact with my opponent's nose. The young man's feet went forward and upward. The contact to the man's face caused his head to snap backward, putting him in a backward somersault. My mind and body were working in unison, and I had never felt so much power. I was totally focused. As the young man landed with his head partially under the bricklayer's scaffold, I was on top of him, kicking him. I kicked most of his teeth out and was doing my best to crush the young man's skull. My thoughts were jumbled. I kept thinking that this man had attacked me with a 2x4, and if I didn't defend myself, he could come after me again. I was in survival mode. The scaffold was in the way, and I was having a difficult time making solid contact. After about four seconds, my two helpers grabbed me, pulling me back. They had heard and seen what was going on, and it took them a few seconds to swing down from the attic through the ceiling joists.

"Leon, it's okay, we got it," they shouted. "We saw the whole thing."

That broke my focus, I took a deep breath and relaxed. The young man on the floor had blood coming out of his nose and his mouth; his lips were bleeding. He had broken and missing teeth. A couple of the tooth fragments had lodged into my tennis shoes. This young man paid a serious price for trying to bully me. After my childhood of abuse from my parents and years of abuse from Mormon bullies and others, I had promised myself that I would never let anyone bully me again.

"Y'all, let me go. I'm okay. Help him get up. We're going to the superintendent's trailer," I said. I picked up the 2x4 and carried it with me. The young man was mostly unconscious but was able to walk a little as the two helpers mostly carried and dragged him to the superintendent's office.

The superintendent was surprised when his door flung open, and I entered with a 2x4 bat along with two other men who were dragging a third.

"What's going on? What the hell happened to him?" The superintendent was incredulous.

"He tried to hit me with this." I handed the superintendent the 2x4 with the whittled-down handle. "We'll be getting back to work."

The superintendent held up a finger as he picked up the phone, indicating that we should wait where we were.

"Yes, this is the superintendent at a construction job site. We need an ambulance. A man has been injured." He provided the address and answered the dispatcher's questions.

Looking at us as he hung up the phone, he said, "Now, tell me what happened."

I explained how I had thwarted this man's attempt to take my saw and level and how this man had come at me with the 2x4.

"I just reacted when I saw him come at me. I didn't mean to beat the crap out of him. I just wanted to protect myself."

"Damn, remind me not to piss you off," the superintendent said with a little laugh in his voice.

My helpers and I went back to work, and before long, we heard the ambulance come for the young man. We kept working until quitting time.

The next day, I showed up for work. The superintendent caught up with me and informed me that word of what had happened had been reported to the main office, and that I was fired for fighting on the job. I again explained to the superintendent what had transpired over the past few days, but it was above the superintendent's pay grade to overrule the home office. He told me to discuss the situation with the vice president of the construction company in Fort Worth. I went home for the rest of the day and called the home office from my house. I explained detail by detail what had transpired. The vice president told me I could go back to work if the superintendent would allow it. The next morning, I drove to the construction site, parked, and walked to the superintendent's trailer. I knocked on the door.

"Come on in," the superintendent called out.

"Look, I am sorry about what happened, but this young man seemed intent on bullying me from day one, hour one," I explained. "You can ask all the men on this job if I have in any way been aggressive or acted mean at any time. If I hadn't defended myself, I would be the one in the hospital today… or worse."

"I understand you had to protect yourself, but it's out of my hands. Did you try to contact the vice president?"

"I spoke with him yesterday afternoon. He told me I could come back to work if you would allow it. I promise you, I will not start anything, but neither will I be pushed around." I finished my declaration.

"I think I understand what happened, and I don't blame you," said the superintendent. "You have always been good at your job. You can come back to work. I would love to have more of you."

But I soon had reason to speak with the superintendent again.

"One of the bricklayers said he thinks he saw that young man around here carrying a pistol. Is it okay if I bring mine to have nearby?" I put it on the line. "I think the bricklayers are just messing with me, but I would like to be prepared just in case."

"No, I don't mind at all," the superintendent agreed. "In fact, if he shows up with a gun and threatens you and you are close to my pickup — that's my old Chevy over there — I have a Ruger Blackhawk .357 Magnum stuffed under the driver's-side seat. Just in case you need it; it is loaded."

I was able to work a few more days with my crew, but we were finishing up the job.

The superintendent told me, "Leon, you've finished all the work we have for you on this phase. We still need a carpenter of your skill to make all the final preparations for the drywall. This phase will be completed by another company, and you can work for them if you want. I've already vouched for you." He was very helpful to me.

"Great, when will that phase be ready?" It was important for me to keep working.

"I'm told materials will be here later today. You can start the new phase tomorrow. The two helpers you have been working with are being assigned to another task. I have some young men from Nicaragua available. I understand you speak Spanish."

I had taken four semesters of Spanish in college. I was eager to meet the new crew and happy to use the language I had worked hard to learn. A few years ago, I had learned a few Spanish words and had worked with a few men from Mexico.

The Nicaraguans showed up the next day even before I arrived. One of the new crew members had been a schoolteacher in Nicaragua. I made friends with him, and my education in Spanish accelerated over the next couple of weeks. The Nicaraguans and I were assigned to install 2-inch-by-2-inch strips on the bottom of the ceiling joists on 12-inch centers for the drywall. We got along fine. I had issues with only a few — those who tried to take advantage of my easy-going personality and generosity.

"Buenos días hombres, listan para trabajen?" (Y'all ready to go to work?) I asked.

"Si, jefe, nosotros listamos."? (Yes sir, we are ready for work.) My Spanish wasn't perfect, but I had learned a lot, and my command of the language impressed the Nicaraguans.

Things were going well, until Friday. My crew and I were informed that we would have to wait until the following week to get paid. This sounded a little fishy, but I had been on many construction jobs and knew sometimes things get a little behind. I explained everything to my new crew. We came back on Monday and continued with the preparation for drywall. Friday came around, and I was told that the contractor we had been assigned to was having some financial issues. I was assured that we would get paid. I explained everything to the crew. We had become friends. Manuelo asked me what we should do.

I explained it the best I could in Spanish. I told them that if they waited to get paid, they might never get paid. I told them that if they left, they would most certainly not get paid. I explained that if we came to work on Monday and sat on our car hoods, that no one would mess with us, and that way we could watch for anybody who came up to take our jobs. For that day and the next the crew and I waited. Each time a new worker showed up, I told the potential replacement that we were not getting paid. Each time, the new person would immediately turn and leave. Of course, the superintendent was watching and saw what was going on, but he was afraid of me, as was everybody on that job because I stood my ground for what was right. The Nicaraguans and I effectively shut down the multimillion-dollar job.

The superintendent came to me and said that I had a phone call and that I could take it in his trailer. I answered the call.

"Hello, Leon, I'm the contractor that you and your crew have been working for. I apologize that I have not been able to get y'all paid yet, but I now have some money and would like to get y'all paid. If I come out there with some money, are you going to kick my ass?" the contractor sounded genuinely concerned.

"Not if you bring enough cash to pay me and my crew for the work we have done."

"How much do I need to bring?" The superintendent had informed the contractor that I was not someone to mess with.

"I'll calculate it and verify the numbers with my crew and get back to you."

I met with my four-man crew of Nicaraguans and discussed the situation and number of hours worked. We came up with some numbers, and I called the contractor. I had taken the liberty of adding a few hours and dollars to compensate for the time my crew and I had to put into getting paid. It had been a hassle that never would have happened had the contractor paid us as promised when we took the job. I figured if the contractor gave me any trouble, I would stomp his ass in the dirt, too.

I gave him the total due. "When can we expect you to deliver?" I asked.

"I'll be there at noon tomorrow. You're not going to kick my ass, are you?" he said.

"Bring cash money, and we will get along just fine," I reassured the contractor.

The contractor brought cash and presented a most meek and humble personality. I accepted the money, and the contractor left. I then met with my Nicaraguan friends and told them I would not be coming back to work on the job. They were all sad, as we had become friends. I paid them for the hours they worked and saw to it that they got a little extra for their time and aggravation. It was never wise to grab a mountain lion by the tail or screw around with me! I stopped by the superintendent's trailer and said goodbye to him.

My luck had changed for the good since my days in Davy Crockett National Forest, even though I still had to deal with bullies and assholes. I was now so much better prepared.

My marriage, however, was not starting off all that great. My wife was suffering from some ailments and had been seeing a doctor. She told me that she needed surgery. As her surgery date approached, she sprang more news on me that gave me serious pause.

"I dropped my classes at the university," she announced. "I'm going to work for a while. I know I said I didn't want children, but I'm feeling different now, and I want to have a baby." Her mother had just visited — her mom's first and last time to come to our house. It seems my black pit bull, Chopper, didn't care much for her. I'm not sure why; maybe he smelled cat on her, as she had cats, and Chopper hated cats. Nevertheless, it wasn't long after my mother-in-law's visit that my wife dropped that bombshell.

"But you said you didn't want to have children," I countered. "I already have two boys, and I love them both, but I don't want to have any more." This was something we'd discussed before marrying.

"I am not sure why, but my feelings have changed," she repeated.

I decided that to make her happy I would concede to the idea of being a father again. I told her we'd try. Despite our best efforts, she did not get pregnant. I thought maybe all the drugs and alcohol I had abused had caused me to be sterile. I thought about getting tested for fertility but kept asking myself why, since I'd been coerced, and the fact remained that I really didn't want any more children. I didn't see my two as often as I wanted to, and another child would take away what little time I had with my sons. I'd always felt guilty about not having done more for my two boys. My boys still visited in the summer, and I saw them on or near their birthdays and around Christmas. I took them to Tae Kwon Do class and taught them as much as I could, given the limited amount of time I had with them. Always, though, I asked them the same two questions: "Where are you going to college," and "What are you going to study?" The boys were in their teens now and growing like weeds. My marriage added a little stress to my relationship with my sons. If I had more children, I was certain that strain would be worse.

I was unsure of my wife's state of mind at this point, but out of the blue, she announced: "I want a horse." I was puzzled, but I agreed to research options.

"When we find a place to keep a horse, we can get one," I told her, adding that we should really both get horses and should look for two stalls to rent.

A friend directed me to a place that seemed promising. Things were coming together, and I began to get excited about getting a couple of horses. Maybe this is what my wife and I needed, an activity that we could do together. Maybe it would help cement our relationship and build mutual trust. But things were strained and strange between us. I'd begun to notice that my wife and her mother would talk quietly, frequently glancing at me. I was getting the strong feeling that my wife's every decision and her ideas of marriage were orchestrated by her mother. I recalled that on our wedding night, she had made an off-hand comment, which, I later recognized, was a warning that this woman was not one to compromise. But at the time, I brushed it off.

I was doing all I could to make the marriage work. We did find stalls and got our horses. One day, a group of us from the stalls decided to go on a trail ride together. Sundance, my horse, always tried to be in front of the pack as the lead horse. Coming back from a two-hour ride, I was riding in front and rode Sundance down into a ditch about five feet deep and twenty feet across. The sides of the ditch were smooth and sloping so one could ride a horse in and out without much trouble. But when I got my horse down to the middle of the ditch, Sundance suddenly decided she wanted to go back. I pulled the reins to the right to go straight, but Sundance resisted, pulling her head around to the left to go back. Suddenly, as I struggled to keep my balance and turn Sundance around, the right rein broke, causing me to lose my balance. I fell off Sundance, and as I hit the dirt, Sundance spun around and headed back the way she had come, stepping on my upper chest. Sundance weighed about 1,100 pounds, and she did some damage. One of the girls on the ride caught Sundance, and I noticed my wife looking at me. She had a strange look on her face, and I'll never forget thinking that she seemed happy to see me hurt. I knew then that our marriage was over.

My fellow rider brought Sundance back, and I managed to get up. I took the remaining rein and walked Sundance about a mile back to the barn. My chest hurt so bad that I didn't think I could have ridden even if I'd had the other rein. I went to the doctor the next day and took Sundance to the sale barn a couple of days later. I had suffered dislocation of a couple of ribs, was given some Percodan (more opioids!) for pain and told to return the next day. The next day the doctor gave me an adjustment and popped my ribs back into place. "OHHHHHH, damn that hurts!" I cried out.

"Leon, that horse stepped on the upper part of your sternum," the doctor said. "That is about six inches from your neck. Do you get what I am saying?"

"Yeah, I got you, Doc," I admitted.

At home, I joined my wife in the kitchen. I dreaded this moment but knew what needed to be said.

"I know you are not happy," I told her. "I have done all that I know how to do to make you happy, but I can do only so much. I think we should file for a divorce. I know a guy who can handle it for us. You take Star, your quarter horse, and the Coupe de' Ville. I'll keep the pickup and the kitchen stuff. Sound fair to you?" I offered.

"That sounds like a fair deal to me; I'm out of here," she readily accepted.

I offered to help her pack, and before long, she was indeed out of there.

This woman was supposed to have been the one. This was the third, and isn't the third one the lucky charm, and wasn't she Irish? It wasn't like I was running around on her, although I did work a lot and spent time at Tae Kwon Do. We separated, agreed on the details, and filed for an amicable divorce. Despite all the things I had accomplished, in the wake of another failed marriage, I felt that old void again in the pit of my stomach.

But my luck held in other areas, as Ronald, one of my old mates from night school, called me and offered me a job.

"I've been working as a draftsman and recently got hired by a new, upstart home building company," Ronald imparted. "They need someone with your skills and knowledge in home building."

"This sounds exciting. Where and when do I need to report for work.?" I was eager to get back on a job.

"Fate, Texas. I'll meet you at the Waffle House in Rockwall for breakfast, and you can follow me to the subdivision there," he said.

The next morning at the Waffle House, Ronald told me that the two guys he was working for, John and Joe, were highly intelligent members of the Mensa Society. One had been with the FBI, and the other had been a maritime adjuster for a British insurance company,

Lloyds of London. The two men had decided that they needed to change their careers.

I followed Ronald to the jobsite and met the owners. They seemed a little slick to be in the home building business, but if they had the money, then I had the time. I was immediately given the title of foreman, and Ronald was to be my helper. I could see right away that none of the men — neither the two owners nor Ronald — knew anything about the home building business in Texas. I doubted that they knew anything at all about running a business of any kind, much less how to build a house. Their plan was to heavily rely on my skills and knowledge to compensate for their utter lack of both.

I went along with their business plan, as this was an opportunity to work, and they agreed to pay my asking price. I was now making more money than I had ever made. The situation quickly exposed the ignorance in this organization. The concept was to purchase a prefab house system and put it together like a Tinker Toy. The exterior walls were foam filled with chipboard facing. The prefabbed walls were four inches thick, eight feet high, and came in different lengths. Each wall was to be carried to its proper place and connected to the other walls and set down astride the bottom plate, which was a wolmanized, or treated, 2x4. The Texas sun or something had warped or damaged the walls, so it was extremely difficult to get the walls set down over the bottom plates. The roof panels were of the same design, Styrofoam, clad with chipboard, except the roof panels were six inches thick. This system was designed somewhere way up North where weather conditions were very different from the way they are in Texas. The structure's basic design could be likened to a beer cooler. Who in the hell would want to live in a beer cooler in Texas in the summer? Unless, of course, it was full of ice and beer. Texas was subject to tornados, drought, severe storm, hail, and high winds. Other than those considerations, it was a great concept. Well, maybe not so great. I asked John, an owner, how much the prepackaged crap cost. I took it on my own to help these geniuses out. I did a cost analysis and presented my findings to the owners. In the meantime, Ronald and I continued to put this crap together. Ronald exposed his ignorance by demonstrating that he did not know the difference between a 2x4 and a 2x6. I let him expose his lack of building knowledge, and it was soon decided that Ronald was not needed anymore. What was this, Dumb, Dumb, and Dumber Custom Homes? I had to wonder.

A house in Texas needs to breathe due to the high humidity in spring and winter, so soon after the finishing touches were put on outside and inside of this house, the windows began sweating — the model home to be used to sell others — now mold began to grow around the inside of windows. Special enhancements had to be made to create an escape for the moisture buildup in this beer cooler. Again, I had to wonder.

In the meantime, while the painters, plumbers, and electricians were finishing, I began building another house. I was now the superintendent and got a raise in pay. My crew and I were completing the framing on the next house when the owners decided to have me build the rest of the houses in the traditional Texas style, using a standard framing package and "stick-building" them.

John then approached me with a new proposition. "Joe and I wondered if you might be interested in coming in on Saturday and Sunday and meeting prospective buyers. If you sell a house, you'll be paid a bonus," he offered.

"Sounds like fun; I'll be here Saturday morning." I thought this might be the beginning of what? — my third career?

Off to a good start, just two hours after I began working my first Saturday, in walked a young man, his wife, and three children.

John nodded at me. Taking the hint, I greeted the family. I invited them to go with me and look at the subdivision, then I invited them to come into the model home and look at some various blueprints and different designs. Unknown to me, they had already picked out a lot, so when they came in to look at the prints, they were looking for a house for that lot. As I visited with the family, the Smiths, I learned that Mrs. Smith had been diagnosed with cancer recently and had been given six months to live.

"I want my wife to have her new house as a Christmas present," Mr. Smith said. "Can you get the house built so we could move in before Christmas?"

A little stunned, I calculated the time to get the house built. "Yes, absolutely. I will get y'all moved in by Christmas." I promised.

We signed contracts, and the wheels were turning. "Holy crap," I thought, "What if I fail in my promise?"

As many had learned before this couple, if you want to get a job done, ask me to do it. Within a few days of completing the paperwork, it started raining. The crews were not able to get even the forms set for the foundation for a couple of weeks, and I desperately needed to get the slab poured. It continued to rain all during construction. The soil in this neighborhood was Houston Black Gumbo, which soaks up water and takes forever to dry out. In the meantime, it is nearly impossible to work in it when it is wet. As the old saying goes "If you stick with Houston Black when it is dry, it will stick with you when it is wet." A man can get five pounds or more of mud on each boot after walking about five steps into this mud.

Finally, I got a break from the rain and got the slab poured, but then it rained again. The lumber truck could not even get off the road to dump the lumber load. Finally, the gumbo dried out enough to get the lumber offloaded onto the property relatively close to the slab.

I had put together a framing crew, not only to save some money for the company but also to ensure that this project got done quickly and accurately. We got the frame up, and I stayed late into the evenings to get as much done as I could as quickly as I could, as the rain and mud had me behind schedule. I was fulfilling the roles of project manager, lead carpenter, and cleanup man. I installed the exterior sheathing by myself, as my crew had wives, children, and other obligations. When all the framework was completed, I stayed late and used lights to lay the decking for the shingles, which were installed a couple of days afterward. "Now, we are ready to rock," I told John. "We'll get the contract house done by Christmas, but it will be very close." I also had other crews and houses under construction.

"Leon, I know you're doing everything possible to get the job done on time. Keep up the good work," John acknowledged.

The house was finished on time, inside and out, so the family could move in.

December 23, 1985, found the team finishing up last-minute tasks to make the home ready for its new family. I had everyone working on this project, whether or not the job was part of the worker's duties. At 10 p.m., we completed the 2x4 and plywood sidewalk to allow the movers to pull up in front of the property, unload furniture, and move it into the house. It was still too muddy to get the concrete driveway and sidewalk poured.

The weather was perfect on Christmas Eve. At 8 a.m., the temperature was about 60 degrees, and the sun was shining. The moving company was busy moving furniture into the house, and by 1 p.m., everything was in the house. The electricians were checking an outlet and switch, but other than that, everything was working perfectly.

The family had been there all morning to supervise the moving and placement of boxes and furniture, and I was done for the day.

Mr. Smith approached me; he was carrying a soft, long gun case.

"Leon, I want to thank you for getting us moved into our new house by Christmas as you promised," he said. "I know we have had more than usual rain for this time of year." He handed me the gun case. It was heavier than I had expected. It had something in it. The confusion showed on my face.

"See what you think of this," Mr. Smith said.

I unzipped the case at the butt end and pulled out a Mossberg, ventilated Rib, 12-gauge pump shotgun with a checkered stock.

"This is really nice; it looks like it's brand new," I said, running my hands over the weapon and admiring its lines.

"I want you to have this, if you like it," Mr. Smith said shyly.

"You don't have to give me presents; this is your gun. I was just doing my job, and I get paid by the company to do a job," I demurred.

"Hey, I came by many a night after dark, and I saw you working with temporary lights on the exterior sheathing, decking, and cleaning up. I want you to have this," the new homeowner insisted.

I could see that the buyer's wife had lost a lot of weight. She had dark circles around her eyes and had been wearing a headscarf to cover her hair loss. My real reward was fulfilling my promise to a dying woman. That was enough for me, but the buyer really wanted me to have the gun.

"Okay," I agreed. Fighting back tears, I gave the man a hug and went inside to check the inside of the house once more. I found Mrs. Smith and gave her a hug and wished her and the family a merry Christmas. The family already had the Christmas tree up in the living room on the brand-new carpet. The room smelled like a new house and Christmas melded together.

I was not only happy for the family, but also that I had pulled the two geniuses, as I was now calling Joe and John, out of a hole, and now the company was profitable. In the meantime, I had been promoted to vice president in charge of operations.

But a different problem had surfaced. This was the mid-1980s, and the savings and loans institutions were going belly up, one after another. The interest rates were soaring to 25 percent and more for construction loans. Money for construction dried up. New housing dried up as well. There would be no more custom or tract home building for the time being.

I contemplated what to do next. I remembered back when I was attending the university, I'd been riding my bicycle home from class when I noticed a small, private aircraft sticking out of the side of a three-story apartment building. I wondered who pays for those repairs. I knew that John had been involved with a few insurance companies during his tenure as an insurance adjuster. The painter on our jobs had also had some experience with insurance repair. I approached John and the painter about doing insurance repair work.

I was also faced with changes in my life outside of work. My first wife had passed away. She had stomach cancer. My boys had been growing and maturing. My older son had been recruited by West Point Military Academy. The questions I had asked the boys over the years — where are you going to school and what are you going to study — were paying off. For now, one of those questions was answered for my older son, Aaron. I was a proud daddy to have a son accepted to West Point. Maybe I had not been the best dad, but I was getting my older son educated, unlike the hillbilly family I had grown up with.

Spring arrived, and I called Aaron. "What would you like to do when you come home for summer vacation?" I asked. I'd had to call at 9 p.m. to a central number as cadets were members of the military and were in class or on duty at various hours.

"I don't care, just whatever you want to do." Aaron was non-committal.

"No, we are going to do what you want to do. What is it you want to do?" I was insistent.

"Well Dad, I would like to go fishing," said Aaron.

I hadn't fished since I was a young boy and fished with my grandfather. I had no tackle nor a boat, and I was never that good a fisherman, anyway.

"No problem, we'll go fishing if that's what you want," I said. "See you next month."

"Dad, when I say I want to go fishing, that means I want to catch some fish," Aaron was laughing now.

"I'll do my best," I promised.

I was terrified. I didn't want to fail in granting my son's wish. I started asking around about a fishing guide, found some information, and called.

The guide told me that he'd been a fishing guide for twelve years. "I won the World Champion Striper Bass Fishing Tournament for two years in a row. I have a very high catch rate. I can tell catching fish is very important to you. I will take you to a tried-and-true area. I will provide the boat, bait, tackle, a cooler of water, and I will clean your catch if you want me to," he said.

He had an opening that fit our schedule. He advised me to bring sunscreen, a hat, rubber-soled shoes, non-alcoholic beverages, and to meet him just south of the Denison Dam in the park. "You'll see my truck with the advertising on it. You may want to bring a change of clothes you would leave in your vehicle in case it rains so you could change into dry clothes before you leave."

It sounded like I had stumbled across the man I needed. I was beside myself. I was sure Aaron would catch some fish!

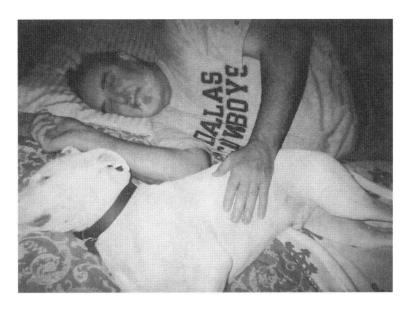

Cruiser, one of my pet pit bulls.

CHAPTER 8

General Contracting, Race Cars, Boys' College Careers

I paid for airline tickets and picked up my older son at the Love Field Airport in Dallas. We went to my house and got ready for the fishing trip we'd take the next day. The excitement was almost palpable. We talked about the trip until late in the night while we played Las Vegas-style Gin Rummy. We woke up the next morning, still excited, had a late breakfast, and at around 7:30, we got into my Ford F-250 pickup.

I handed Aaron a map.

"You are the navigator," I told him.

He unfolded the map, and using the index, found the address.

"Turn right at this corner," Aaron pointed.

After about a two-hour drive, we arrived at Denison Park on the Red River. We immediately spotted a pickup with fishing advertising on its side. A man with blonde hair and dressed in jeans and a red and black plaid shirt got out and met us at the back of his truck.

We made introductions.

"Y'all ready to catch some fish?" he asked. "I'll get the bait and gear loaded. Bring anything you brought down to the dock."

"Aaron, I bet you a dollar that I will catch the biggest fish," I lightheartedly challenged Aaron.

"It's a bet," Aaron said, accepting my challenge.

The guide called back to us, instructing us to don life jackets and board the boat, which was a 20-foot airboat docked nearby.

I suddenly envisioned us sitting in the boat with our lines in the water, not getting any bites. I was beginning to worry that Aaron might not have a good time.

The guide returned, and we pushed off. As we got out on the Red River, our guide reviewed the things we needed to know. We turned upriver toward Denison Dam. We could see the water pounding over the forty-foot-high spillway, frothing high into the air. There was a mist hanging over the area. The guide piloted the airboat into the white water. As he maneuvered the airboat into position, he cast the bait for both Aaron and me and handed a rod and reel to each of us.

Just seconds later, Aaron called out excitedly. "I got one!"

"Keep the line taut as you real in. Don't lose it," the guide shouted over the roar of the water.

"I got one too, son," I immediately countered.

Aaron pulled back on the rod, reeling as he moved the rod forward, keeping the line taut. When he got his catch up to the side of the airboat, the guide used a fishing net and scooped up the fish. Shortly after, he netted my catch.

"Mine's bigger," Aaron boasted with a huge grin on his face.

"We'll see when we are finished who catches the biggest one," I said. "Give it time."

We fished until about noon. The striped bass were thick as flies on a fresh cow patty, and every time the guide took us into the white-water and cast the lines, Aaron and I pulled in another large striper. By around noon we had caught our limit, which was five stripers each. Aaron caught a striper that measured twenty-nine inches, one-half inch longer than my biggest catch. I wanted to celebrate seeing my son's wish fulfilled, spending a fun day together, and conceding the one-dollar bet to Aaron.

"Y'all take a break and get a hamburger," suggested the guide. "Come back in an hour, and I'll bait the hooks with a different bait, and we'll catch some catfish."

Aaron had been excited about fishing and catching the largest striper of the day. I didn't think he could be any more excited until I saw the look on his face when he realized we'd be fishing for catfish, too.

After lunch, we boarded the airboat and fished for another hour or two. The guide then called it a day and maneuvered the boat over to the fish-cleaning station. We watched as the guide cleaned and fileted the fish and put them in plastic bags full of water. I wrote the guide a check, which included a generous tip. Aaron and I loaded up the pickup and made the two-hour drive back to my house.

We laughed and talked about the fishing trip for days, until Aaron had to return to West Point.

For me, it was back to work as usual.

The new contracting company that John had formed was functioning at only a very basic level. One of the problems that people had when coming from a large corporation was adjusting to a small business environment. John had handled maritime claims for Lloyds of London and others as an insurance adjuster. Large corporations provide pens, paper, computers, and training on how and when to use them. In a small business, it is frequently a fly-by-the-seat-of-your pants operation. John applied the rules and procedures as if he were running a multi-million-dollar company, but this company was struggling to get off the ground. John was lost, and I did not have the knowledge or expertise to help him out. I was not experienced in the business side, although I did know that to succeed, revenues had to exceed expenses. I paid a visit to John.

As I entered John's office, John's feet were up on his desk, and he was leaning back, watching a TV that was on the cabinet across from his desk. This was how I usually found John.

"Hey Leon, I'm glad you came in. I have a project for you," he said. "I want you to work with a computer programmer to design a computer-generated construction estimating program."

While I found this idea compelling, I didn't want to show John my excitement. "Well," I said calmly. "I guess I could do that. But John, if you are bored, you could try selling jobs or come out and work with me. Get a better understanding of home building and repair."

"Why would I want to do that?" he asked.

"It would help with your bottom line. And you look bored."

"It's not going to happen," said John.

"You realize you are not helping your own company. This is a small upstart company that needs all the help it can get. Even if you sold only one house a week or one repair job a week, that would improve your net profits dramatically."

"Up yours," said John. "What did you come in for anyway?"

"I came to review where we are on our current projects."

"Then get to it."

John was taking a salary but producing nothing, and this was killing this small upstart business. While my concerns about the business remained, I had begun working with the computer programmer to design a construction estimating program.

I had made a lot of headway on the project when John had to call it quits because there was not enough production, and expenses were too high.

I needed to make a change. By now I had learned a little about the policies and procedures in the insurance claims business. I found this very interesting, so I decided to start a company of my own and run it out of my house to keep expenses down.

I formed a corporation and marketed home repair and remodeling. I had met a few adjusters I could call on, hoping to get a referral to repair someone's damaged home. Working with adjusters was the only way I knew to market my business at that time. I called on my own insurance agent for a reference or two, and I got a couple of names and telephone numbers of adjusters in the property claims business.

My insurance agent referred me to an adjuster who had about thirty years' experience. This adjuster, Gordon, soon learned how persistent I was, and he began to have a little confidence in me. On the other hand, I recognized the value of getting a good report from the insured when Gordon referred me.

"Leon, how much do you pay these people to call me and brag on you?" Gordon joked.

I laughed. "Gordon, I know that you get a lot of complaints for different reasons. When an insured tells me, 'Thank you for doing a good job,' I thank them and tell them how much I appreciated them allowing me to make the repairs to their home. I also tell them that had it not been for you, I would have not been sent to meet them. I also tell them that if they have the time and desire, to call you and thank you, as you are always having to listen to unhappy people. I tell them that it might be nice for you to hear from a satisfied customer." I recognized a valuable business contact when I had one.

Committed to doing the job right, I staffed the best carpenters, painters, and roofers I could find. I worked long hours and weekends to get my jobs done on time and to build a solid reputation for quality and integrity. As a result, Gordon taught me a lot about the insurance claims business from an adjuster's perspective. I learned quickly, and it wasn't long before I was accepted by Gordon's insurance claims group and became a preferred contractor for them and a few other claims groups as well.

After a couple of years, I had built a small but well-known contracting company and had established a reputation of honesty and integrity. I had also become a trainer by default. A few of the companies would get a new adjuster or an adjuster from another specialty group who transferred to the property group and got assignments to handle property claims. I would take the newbie out on a roof claim or a water damage claim. I taught them how to measure roofs and assess the items needed to repair water damage. The adjusters got their policy education through their company.

I got a call and was assigned an insured to contact. It was an elderly woman I'd been instructed to take care of. I had just hired a new carpenter and decided to let the newbie handle the job as it was a small, relatively simple water damage claim to the floor by the refrigerator.

I gave him the address and the keys to the cargo van. "This is an older woman, so be patient and explain everything to her. Here is a list of materials and a list of things you might need and that need to be done. Be sure to get all the rotted wood out and put new wood back so that it's as good as, or better than new. Be sure and put plywood over any holes so she doesn't fall through the floor and get hurt," I instructed.

The newbie returned after he inspected the damages.

"So, what do you think?" I asked him.

"I can pull out the water-damaged plywood and scab some new floor joists. She won't know if I replaced all the rotted subfloor underneath. It will save some money," he said.

"I think you misunderstand me," I said. "I want to make sure that one hundred percent of all the rotted wood is taken out, and I want you to put it back like new construction or better." I was thinking about the things my grandfather had taught me. "Always do your best, and never, ever shirk your duties!"

"No, no, no, we can save some money," the new carpenter insisted.

I couldn't believe what I was hearing. Here was this new carpenter arguing with me before he even got to his first assignment. My temper had been in check for quite some time, but my blood was beginning to boil. How dare this new hire try to cheat a customer, much less a helpless older lady? If something like this should happen and was discovered, it would damage my reputation severely. Besides, I never operated like that, anyway. It was blatantly obvious that I had made a mistake in hiring this carpenter.

"Give me the keys to the van," I demanded. "It's obvious that we have very different philosophies about how to repair houses. I'll get someone else to handle this job."

The carpenter started to hand me the keys, and when I reached out to take them, the carpenter suddenly pulled them back. This infuriated me. I looked up to my left as though something was coming at me, which caused the carpenter to look up and to his right to see what I was looking at. I hit him on the left side of his jaw with a reverse punch (Tae Kwon Do term), or what is commonly known as a right-handed punch. The carpenter's knees buckled as his body went limp, and he went down, unconscious. I reached down, retrieved my keys and the paperwork.

As the carpenter regained consciousness, shook his head, and began to stand, I said to him,

"You're fired, asshole."

I had other skilled craftsmen working for me, so it was just a matter of getting another technician to take care of this small and simple, but important, job. I took every job seriously no matter how small or big.

Not long after that incident, a large hailstorm hit, and it was all hands on deck. Lots of insurance companies and claims groups were now calling on me to do the first inspections on roofs. The agreement was that I would inspect the roof, take photos, draw a diagram of the roof, and turn in an estimate for repairs, or in the case of hail damage, how much it would cost to replace the shingles. This was particularly important because there were a lot of adjusters who could not calculate the squares on a simple single offset roof, so they certainly could not handle a cut-up roof with multiple offsets or a steep roof. If I got the job to do the repairs, I would not bill the insurance claims department for the inspection. If I did not get the job, the claims department would pay me for my expenses, which ranged from $75 to $125 per inspection. This was a win-win scenario; I made a lot of money, and the claims departments saved a lot of money. My reputation for quality and integrity continued to spread. To stay close to these adjusters, I treated a lot of them to lunch, and I purchased Cowboys season tickets so I could treat my favorite adjusters to football games. I had also bought a beautiful 1,800-square-foot brick home in the northwest portion of Dallas, inside the 635 Loop.

Several years before this, I'd begun setting annual goals, and now every year I raised the bar. Each year I would meet or exceed the previous year's goals. I got so busy I decided to sell my dirt track race car, my 1965 Harley XLCH Sportster, and my 1965 Mercury Comet. These were "man toys" that I no longer had any interest in nor had time for.

I had developed an interest in racing. A few years before, a neighbor had asked me if I would be interested in driving his race car at Kennedale Raceways. This was a quarter-mile dirt track near Fort Worth. I had jumped at the chance; I loved fast cars and hot rods. After I had driven the car in two different races on two different nights, I decided to not drive my neighbor's car anymore, as it was poorly built and dangerous. When going into corners at more than seventy miles per hour, the car would rock like a small boat in the Gulf of Mexico during a storm.

My race friend, Dick, feared that I would be killed driving what he called "that hunk of junk."

"So, what do you do to your cars to make the cars safe?" I asked.

"Come by the shop and I'll show you," Dick offered.

I went to Dick's transmission shop the following week.

I thanked him for letting me come and explained that I didn't have a race car of my own. I knew I needed a hobby to use up some of my surplus energy and to fill a void. A hobby would also keep my mind occupied.

"I can help you build your own car if you like," Dick offered. "If you get a tire sponsor, a radiator sponsor, and a wrecking yard sponsor, it won't cost much to build a car. You can use one of my open bays and build it here. I'll coach you." This sounded perfect.

I loved muscle cars and had always wanted to race. I had done a little drag racing with my brother-in-law's '66 Mustang, but I had rarely won. The car had a three-speed manual transmission, a 289 ci V-8 motor with a three-quarter race cam, a Carter four-barrel carburetor, and dual exhausts. That sounded great, but it wasn't all that fast compared to the competition that showed up on Friday and Saturday nights at the out-of-town and highly illegal drag strip.

I began building a 1977 Chevelle with a 350 ci motor that the wrecking yard provided. Dick coached me, and we built the car, roll cage, and drive train specifically to race quarter-mile dirt tracks. The ring and pinion gears were welded together to get Positraction 100 percent of the time. I bought a 350 four-bolt main engine block from a motor rebuild shop and used the other motor as a core deposit, and the salvage yard sponsor donated the bowtie heads. We took the heads to a machine shop to be shaved, ground, and prepared for racing. A special, reground, General Motors cam was used as original equipment, as competitors who were racing a Chevy and competing in the Street Stock Class had to use all GM parts. We used a two-barrel carburetor where the smaller jets were taken out, and we used some of the largest jets made for that carburetor. The grind on the cam, the work on the heads, and the carburetor allowed for this motor to produce more than 350 horsepower. We had stripped the car of all the glass and nonessentials which made it much lighter. Installed on the steering column was a tachometer that had a recall function. With these motors, the driver could run up to about 6,500 rpm on a quarter-mile track with a three-speed, manual transmission that was locked in first gear. With the manual transmission locked in first gear, the car would reach speeds up to or possibly a little more than 80 mph on a quarter-mile track, while running 6,500 rpm, registering in the memory on the tachometer. The tach had a recall function, so that after any race, anybody could push the recall button and see what the maximum rpm was for the motor in the previous race. There was no time for shifting gears, as the track was too short, so basically, the strategy was, "foot on the gas," and don't even think about using the brakes. The front brakes had been disabled just in case the driver forgot Rule No. 1: "Do not use brakes while racing on a dirt track." I soon moved to a three-eighth mile NASCAR-sanctioned track after getting my NASCAR license on my first application. My 1977 Chevelle also passed the NASCAR inspection.

The salvage company that sponsored me was now offering me a '74 Nova. I had learned that when I raced on nights when the Dirt South Group raced, the racers left deep ruts down low and inside on the turns. The Nova had leaf springs that gave it a lot more stability side to side than the coil-spring suspension that was standard factory setup on the Chevelle.

My football knees had been irritating me a lot, and I had finally gotten the stars to line up so I could get surgery on my knees. My primary care physician had recommended an orthopedic surgeon. I had contacted the surgeon to see what kind of a deal I could make with him. He said he owned a four-plex in Arlington, and it needed a new roof. We discussed details, and the bottom line was that I would replace the hail-damaged roof on his four-plex, and he would remove bone fragments and repair ligament damage. During the few weeks that I was recovering from arthroscopic knee surgery, I had let my best mechanic helper, Bill, drive the Chevelle.

Changing the length of the track from one-quarter mile to three-eighths of a mile presented a different challenge for gearing, which included rpm, transmission, third-member rear end, and motor. One could even change the rim size on the rear wheels and use either fourteen-inch or fifteen-inch rims. Tire profile could be changed slightly on the tires as well, but for the "stock" class, this was a little over the top and cost more money.

Bill had run a few races, and I'd watched him. I advised: "Bill, if you want to win a race, you have to finish!"

Bill grinned. "All right. I'll try to stay out of the pileups."

"You also need to quit running into the side of the #17 car," I further cautioned.

"Yeah, I know, but she pisses me off," said Bill.

"You cannot possibly win a race if you do not finish! Do you understand that?" I was adamant.

"Yes, sir, I will stay out of wrecks."

But after six weeks on the NASCAR track, I knew I had to make a change for Bill.

"I think we've worn out our welcome here with you being in a wreck every freaking race, so I'm moving our race schedule to The Devil's Bowl." I told him. "We'll be running a half-mile track there. The top speed will be around 100 mph or more there, and I think that would really be a lot of fun. We're going to use a four-speed manual transmission and lock it in second gear. That will be perfect gearing for the longer track." I went to the wrecking yard, explained the situation to my sponsor, and picked up a four-speed transmission.

While Bill was racing, my group and I had been getting the Nova ready. Because I had experience building the Chevelle, the build on the Nova had a more defined strategy and I had a much better vision of what the final product would look like. This was an improved build.

My small team and I were now ready for Devil's Bowl Speedway in Mesquite, Texas. The tow truck that I designated to pull the race cars was a Chevrolet dually painted two-tone in tan and dark brown. I painted my new race car tan and brown to match the tow truck, and I labeled my car #41, as I had just had my forty-first birthday. I was heading to the race confident in my Nova. With the leaf spring suspension on the rear, I could tell the car was more stable and would run a lot smoother when running down low in the turns after the open-wheeled, Dirt South, Outlaws race.

I paid my dues and received a membership to the Dirt South organization. My knees had been healing, and I was ready to drive again. People talk about carburetors, intakes, valves, heads, cam-shafts, etc. but when the green flag drops it was all bullshit in the shop. The butterflies fill your stomach as everybody stomps on the gas pedal, the wheels are spinning, and the open exhausts from these hopped up motors make a loud roar, in an effort to get to the front.

Traditionally, track management watered down the packed dirt track just before the first race to keep the dust to a minimum, so the first race on any given night was usually muddy and very slippery. If the car and driver did well in the first race, then they were invited to race the second race, called a trophy race. This race consisted of the top five cars in the first race. Then the third and final race would be a twelve-lap, six-mile race. The mud on the track would be drying up and getting tacky at this point. The cars had the softest rubber tires they could afford, and they were used to achieve maximum grip on the dirt. The tires on the "street stock" class must have a Department of Transportation (DOT) label and approval.

I was pretty experienced at driving the mud. Having grown up in the country, I was used to the challenge of driving on muddy roads after a hard rain. If a driver didn't know how to maneuver in the mud, he could get stuck in the middle of a road. My experience made me a natural for driving a race car on mud and dirt. I won enough races and money to help pay for most of my expenses for what was my passion at the time. The actual car cost very little money, but the time required to have a car ready to race every week took basically every night and all day Saturday, sometimes Sunday.

After going through my last divorce, the race car had been good therapy for me, and I really enjoyed it. I was having success at the various tracks and could recall only one night when things went a bit awry. We were at a NASCAR track. The #1 car, a White Monte Carlo, seemed to have my #41 car on its tracking device that night. The only way the #1 car could keep up with my #41 car was by getting close enough in the turns to bump it. The #1 car became somewhat unstable when bumped, and running approximately 100 miles an hour on dirt made it difficult to control. After the races were over each night, the top finishers usually stopped by the pay window on the way out. The crew for the #1 car pulled up close to me. My crew wasn't around when I shouted to the #1 crew.

"You assholes can't win anything without using dirty tricks!" I yelled at them.

"Oh yeah? Come get some of this, shithead!" was the response. In Tae Kwon Do, I had learned to defend myself against four or more aggressors. This might be fun!

I started toward the crew as they bailed out of their truck. They went in different directions and as I approached the driver of the #1 car, one of the crew had run around another car and had come up behind me. I felt a tap on the back of my head, and as I turned around to face the attacker, he ran like the coward he was. I went back toward the driver, and he ran also. The third crew member had a military-style haircut and stood his ground. I took a couple of steps toward the third one, and as I got close enough, I struck him in the groin with a front kick. It was off target slightly, and the bullseye was really small and difficult to hit. The third crew member ran also, knowing he was outmatched. That was the last time I would race at the NASCAR track. I liked the racers and crews better at the Devil's Bowl.

I was able to drive again, and my crew and I began our quest for the #1 spot at the Devil's Bowl Speedway. After quite a few weeks, I was really getting the hang of the half-mile dirt track and was doing well. One night, my Nova was really hooking up, and I was outrunning everybody; in fact, I finished first in the final race.

I was instructed to bring my car up front after the race. This was about halfway down the track between turn four and turn one. This positioned me in the center and in front of the stands and the spectators.

The track announcer at The Devil's Bowl spoke: "Leon, this must be your night; you won two of the three races tonight."

"I just want to thank my crew and my sponsors who have supported me," I said into the microphone. "This is a great and humbling experience. My car was hooking up just like you draw it up." The Devil's Bowl Queen presented me with a trophy and the queen and I had our photo taken together with my car and the trophy. After all the hoopla, I drove my car back to the pits, where I found numerous fans lined up to get my autograph. This was one of my proudest moments, rivaling the first-place trophy from the 20th Annual Texas State Karate championships.

My business was also going very well. My contracting company had been getting busier and busier, and by this time I had sold all my "toys," including my race cars. It was time to build the company and, I hoped, enhance my lifestyle. I had grown tired of working every night on the car and dedicating my time to race cars and racing. I felt the need to settle down and refocus. I had bought a home that needed some attention, and I wanted to spend some time pursuing other things. My longtime friend Dep had suggested that I take up scuba diving a long time ago.

He had helped me when I was recovering from double knee surgery. I had a little extra money and knew how much Dep liked scuba diving. In fact, Dep and another friend were avid scuba divers. Both friends had encouraged me to learn, so I called Dep. Now that I had some spare time, I called him to discuss lessons.

I told Dep I had a deal for him: "If you'll teach me scuba, I'll pay for the airfare to get us to Cozumel, Mexico, and I'll pay for the hotel rooms for a four-day weekend. What do you say?"

"Hell yes!" was his response. "I'll get some tanks and equipment, and I'll begin teaching you the basics in my friend's swimming pool. How soon will you be ready?"

Dep promised to have the gear ready by that coming weekend.

True to his promise, he did. He also gained permission for us to use his friend's swimming pool.

"Hey Dep, this is easier than I thought," I told him after trying out the gear. "When do you want to go to Cozumel?" I took to scuba diving easily and was eager to get out of the swimming pool and into the ocean.

"Crap, Leon, if you are paying airfare and hotel, just tell me when and where, and I'll adjust my schedule." Dep was enthusiastic.

My birthday was coming up in November, which was off-season for tourists in Cozumel. Because of this, hotel rates were lower than usual, and airline tickets were cheaper than usual. I met with a travel agent and made reservations for a four-day weekend in Cozumel for Dep and me. Like my childhood, Dep's early years were spent in poverty. Dep had grown up in the city and, like me, wanted to make something out of life, something more than simply and blindly following the Mormon way of life. Dep stood about six feet tall. He had blonde hair and blue eyes. He had been a competitive swimmer in high school, ranking in the top three in the state of

Texas in his respective competition, so he was an excellent swimmer. I felt safe to be swimming in the Caribbean with Dep, as he was well trained and able. I also trusted Dep, even though I felt I had been betrayed by my other Mormon friends. Dep and I had met in the Mormon church many years ago, and although we were not really that close, Dep always kept up with me. It was mostly because of my mistrust of the Mormons that I had kept my distance. I did not trust any Mormons anymore. But Dep had always offered friendship and had supported me at various times during our distant relationship. Dep had also gone through a divorce. His first wife and he had been married and sealed in the Mormon Temple, which meant for all time and eternity. Dep's wife had had an affair with one of Dep's business associates, which resulted in his divorce. His wife had given birth to seven children. Dep questioned how many of those seven children were really his.

November came and Dep and I flew to Cozumel, an island east of the mainland of Mexico and east of the well-known city of Cancun, which is on the northern tip of the Yucatan Peninsula. We checked into the Plaza of the Americas, a hotel on the west coast of Cozumel. Dep checked out the options for renting scuba gear and made arrangements for us to go diving the next day. Rather than pay for a "boat dive trip," which was big business in Cozumel, Dep planned for us to enter the water from the beach. This was great except for two things: I had had double knee surgery a few months earlier, and there was a strong current that neither Dep nor I was aware of. The current ran at thirty to sixty feet below the surface and flowed from south to north. When we entered the water and began swimming near the bottom, the current was hardly noticeable as we were swimming south to north with the current. The difficulty began when we turned around and began to swim south against the current. My knees were still weak from the surgery, and my legs began to fatigue rather quickly. Dep, with his great experience in the water, motioned for me to dive a little deeper and swim along the bottom. Dep then showed me how to use my hands to dig into the sandy bottom and use my arms to help propel myself southward. We covered enough distance to the south and far enough east so that we could exit the water and re-enter the beach just north of the hotel. It was a little scary at first, but Dep had a solution, and all went well. I learned a valuable lesson about the water and currents around Cozumel. I returned to Cozumel on dive trips a few years later. My time spent with Dep had proved to be valuable. In addition, the bond had been strengthened between us. The second day of our trip, Dep approached me.

"Leon, do you have any specific plans for today?" he asked.

"No, my knees are sore from yesterday, and I thought I might refrain from swimming today," I said.

"I have an idea," Dep said. I'll be back in a little while."

He came back with tickets for a water shuttle/ferry that transported people to and from Cozumel to Playa Del Carmen, which was just south of Cancun. Later that morning we loaded onto the shuttle and traveled to Playa Del Carmen. Dep found a car rental office, rented a Volkswagen Beetle, and picked up a map of the west coast of the Yucatan Peninsula. Dep drove, and I navigated. We came to a crossroads in the middle of the jungle and stopped for a minute to study the map. Out from the jungle came a small, young girl who looked to be of Mayan descent. She may have been seven or eight years old. She offered to sell us a bag of oranges. Neither of us spoke her version of Spanish, but we were able to figure out that she wanted three dollars for the bag of fruit. We checked our cash on hand, and neither of us had any small bills. Dep gave her a twenty-dollar bill as she handed him a small bag of oranges. She looked at the twenty, turned and hauled ass back into the jungle on a dead run. We waited for a few minutes, turned and looked at each other and burst out laughing. There was no way this little girl had change; in fact, twenty dollars would probably feed her family for a month or two. She was not coming back. We continued our journey south. After a while we arrived at our destination, Chichén Itzá, a well-known Mayan ruin. It had become a tourist destination, and it was one of the most interesting things I had ever seen. After visiting that site, we proceeded to Tulum's Castle, which was another Mayan ruin that sat on the east coast of the Yucatan on an elevated area a few hundred feet above sea level, overlooking the Caribbean Sea. This was a truly spectacular place to visit. My knees were getting tired and sore, so after the personally guided tour, we traveled back to Playa Del Carmen and caught the shuttle back to Cozumel. I felt gratified, as I had done something nice for my friend Dep, and in the meantime, I had learned a whole lot. It was time to go back to work, so we caught our flight back to Texas.

I had been feeling lonely. I had had girlfriends and lovers but never felt fulfilled. There was something missing in my life. I thought it might be religion as I was raised with beliefs based on God and Christianity. I began checking out some other Christian-oriented religions and found Unity Church. The church had a truly gifted spiritual leader who provided spiritual messages for his congregation. This group had a vastly different approach to spiritualism. Heaven and hell were for the most part left out of the sermons and teachings. I began attending the class offered each Sunday for single people and eventually began attending the main service. The preacher used the Bible to provide spiritual messages but left out all the talk of sinners, hellfire, and damnation, and talk of the devil. I was not getting that message of guilt that the Mormons constantly threw at its members. In fact, the Unity Church allowed for sin as it was common for man to err. It was okay to divorce; it was okay to make mistakes. It was a philosophy about 180 degrees off Mormonism. The sermons always made me think about how the topic as it pertained to my life. I made new friends, and life got better for a while.

Business had gotten better as well. I had grown my company, bought a nice house, and had joined a gym where I exercised regularly. I also began attending a Kung Fu school for stretching as well as exercise and learned more about another philosophy in the martial arts. My instructor kept after me to test for more advanced belts, as I had been wearing a white belt, signifying a beginner. My Tae Kwon Do instructor had granted me an honorary black belt. When it came to sparring, I never felt threatened by any of the students. I was there for myself and no one else. I told the instructor that I felt that I had enough belts but would like to attend for the stretching and exercise. After a while I got tired of my instructor trying to get me to take the belt test, so I quit going to class.

I was focusing on work. One of my favorite adjusters called me to give me a name, a phone number, and address to a claim. The adjuster told me, "Take care of this customer." I called the insured and made an appointment to inspect the water damage to his bathroom.

"Hello, Mr. Graham," I introduced myself. "I received a call from your adjuster. He tells me that you have a small problem with some plumbing in your bathroom. When would be a good time for me to come by and take a look at it?"

Mr. Graham told me that he and his wife were retired, so I could come by at my convenience. "Just let us know ahead of time so we can be prepared," he said.

"How about tomorrow morning around 10?" I offered. I knew that they were older, and my experience had shown me that older people are at their best in the mornings.

"We look forward to meeting with you," Mr. Graham replied.

I arrived a little before 10 a.m. Mr. Graham and his wife lived in a somewhat exclusive, high-end neighborhood in north Dallas. The house was a 1942 model, Greek Mediterranean architectural-style home that sat on almost a half-acre. Just on the west side of the main road near the Grahams' residence was where cosmetics guru Mary Kay and President-to-be George W. Bush had owned homes and had lived. This was a small part of what was referred to by real estate agents in Dallas as "The Golden Corridor." Mr. Graham had served as executive vice president of a Texas-based insurance company, where he had been in charge of the life insurance division. Their homeowner policy was with the same company, but of course, was in the property division. Mr. Graham was a well-liked and respected popular leader. Upon meeting him, I immediately recognized him to be a true Southern gentleman and a true professional.

I arrived and knocked on the front door. Mr. Graham opened the door, and we exchanged greetings. Mr. Graham invited me to come in and inspect the damage. As we entered the spare bathroom on the way into the bathroom, I immediately saw the problem, which was a very common problem with shower stalls. The shower pan had been leaking, and the plaster behind the ceramic tile had become saturated with water. The tile had started coming loose and falling off the wall. Shower pans always fail; it's just a matter of when and how bad. The average life expectancy for a shower pan is seven years.

"Mr. Graham, I see the problem and have repaired numerous shower pans over the years. I'll get a crew out here and get started removing the damaged and rotted wood. I'll come by and bring some

tile samples so you can pick out the color and style for the new tile."
I reviewed the process to solve the problem.

Mr. Graham and I communicated effectively and developed an unusually close relationship rather quickly. The shower repair went smoothly and quickly. After the repairs were completed, I went by to do a final inspection and collect for the work.

"I have something I would like for you to look at for me, please," Mr. Graham said.

He led me to the opposite end of the long house into the formal dining room, which was about sixty feet from the guest bathroom. Mr. Graham pulled the draperies back from the front window. At the base of the wall, the oak hardwood floor was rotted through, as was the subfloor. The water had been leaking through the roof at the stoop over the window for years but had gone unnoticed because the draperies covered the hole caused by the ongoing leak. The Grahams, getting older, rarely entered the formal dining room.

I told Mr. Graham that I would take a few photos, get them to his insurance adjuster, and review the coverage. "I'll get back to you soon," I promised.

The next day I met with the adjuster. Again, I was instructed to take care of Mr. Graham. and the adjuster assured me that the insurance company would cover the cost of repairs, less the deductible. I also informed the adjuster that this was going to be an expensive repair as the wallpaper was a thirteen-color mural that had been manufactured in France. The same pattern was no longer available. This meant that the wallpaper had to be run through the process thirteen times, once for each color. Not only was the neighborhood high-end, but this also was by far the most expensive wallpaper I had ever encountered. Not only was the product expensive, but it also took a technician with special skills to install it properly.

I told the adjuster that I'd researched the wallpaper and that the exact print had been discontinued many years before. "Mr. and Mrs. Graham have picked out a wallpaper of like kind and quality," I told him. "It will cost $250 a roll to purchase and install it. It cannot be purchased through a regular paint and wallpaper dealer; I have to purchase it through an exclusive dealer in the arts district near downtown Dallas."

The adjuster told me to do what was needed.

I visited the Grahams to review my findings. I advised them that it would take a few days after ordering the wallpaper to get it in.

"Leon, we were paid for some hail damage a few years ago. It didn't seem to be serious, so we waited. I put the money for the roof repair in an account so when the time came, we would have the money to replace the roof. Would you be interested in replacing our shingles?"

I happened to have shingle samples on hand, as I did a lot of roof replacements in the area. I told Mr. Graham: "I have specialty crews for roofs and could probably have a crew out this week and replace the shingles. We'll need to pay special attention to the galvanized flashing around the stoop as that is where the leak in the dining room came from."

We replaced the roof and flashing that week, and a few days later, the wallpaper came in. Part of the dining room damage was to the virgin oak flooring. I had a specialty wood floor crew, and they were able to feather in the repairs so I had to replace only a small area of the wood floor. Then they had to sand and finish the oak floor, which ran all the way down to the master bedroom door. It looked like a new floor when my crew had finished.

The crews had performed each repair as well as could be hoped for and were finishing up the assignments when I went by for an inspection.

I asked Mr. Graham if was pleased with the work.

"Leon, you and your crews have performed like true professionals, and we truly appreciate you and the members of your crews. Would you mind looking at something else for us?"

Mr. Graham took me into the master bedroom and pointed to the ceiling. I said to him to please come over here and wait for me in the hallway and I will be right back.

I excused myself to gather my tape measure and my camera. I measured the distance from floor to ceiling at each corner of the room and measured at the center of the room, again from floor to ceiling.

"The distance in the center of the room suggests that the ceiling is sagging about three inches," I explained. "I'm going to my warehouse and get a couple of things and will return in an hour or two. In the meantime, I want you and Mrs. Graham to stay out of the bedroom. Will you do that?"

I picked up three eight-foot pieces of lumber and a few tools from my warehouse and drove back to the Grahams' residence.

I told Mr. Graham that, for safety reasons, I would install a temporary brace in the middle of the bedroom until I could get more information about the cause. I told him I'd also check coverage with his adjuster in the event the problem was what I suspected it was.

"I think I know what's going on, but I need to inspect a little deeper and shoot more photos for the adjuster," I explained. "Where is your attic access?" I wanted to get this right the first time.

I placed a piece of lumber on the floor, laying it flat, and measured it again. I measured and marked the lumber and cut two more pieces to form a "T" and nailed them together. I had cut the length correctly so that I could wedge the "T" between the piece of lumber on the floor and the ceiling, thereby creating a brace to ensure that the ceiling did not experience total failure. I drove a couple of nails in the vertical piece of lumber and asked Mr. Graham for a couple of old towels to hang on the vertical brace.

I explained that I was placing the towels on the brace because I knew that he and Mrs. Graham were not used to having an obstruction in the middle of their bedroom. "They're hanging there as a reminder that this brace is there. I'm going into the attic now to inspect further and take photos for your adjuster," I told him.

In the attic, I found exactly what I had suspected: more water damage! The house was more than fifty years old and was showing it. Looking up from the bedroom, one could see only a finished ceiling but from the attic, I was able to determine the materials used in construction.

I explained to Mr. Graham that the ceiling was sagging from a very slow leak that had been coming in through the old flashing that we replaced at the half gable when we replaced the shingles. The ceiling was a metal lathe and plaster construction, creating a very, very, heavy design. The fasteners that hold the metal lathe had rusted due to a little bit of moisture here and there. The fasteners were rotted out worse towards the center of the room.

"The entire ceiling will need to be replaced," I told him. "I'll get with your adjuster to review photos and coverage. You and Mrs. Graham may need to stay in a hotel for a few days while we repair the ceiling."

"It sounds like there will be some painting necessary," said Mr. Graham. "We wonder if you would paint our living room and sunroom while your painters are here."

Since the first repair was made, Mr. Graham had begun talking to me about purchasing their property. They had lived in the house for thirty-five years and were making final preparations to move into an assisted-living community.

"I have offered this property to you as you are the best choice to own it," Mr. Graham told me. "We have a number of realtors who are friends of ours, but if we choose one to handle the sale of our property, we will offend the others."

"Please understand how much I appreciate your willingness to deal straight with me in the sale of your house, but I cannot afford a property of this quality in this neighborhood," I said. "Besides, I have a beautiful three-bedroom, brick home built in 1958. It has a swimming pool, beautiful trees, and is on a half-acre lot. What would I do with this house? As you know, I am single. Your house is nearly 2,500 square feet. I would be lost in it. I don't see how I could afford this property anyway." I was overwhelmed by the offer.

I reviewed the photos with the Grahams' adjuster and prepared an estimate for the cost of repairs. The adjuster reviewed the scope and pricing and agreed to my estimate. We made the repairs; completed the painting, and I got paid again. The house and detached garage now had new shingles; the interior of the house had refinished oak floors, a new ceiling in the master bedroom, and new paint in the living room, sunroom, and dining room along with the new wallpaper. The interior and roof looked really nice. I had made a solid friendship during this rather lengthy ordeal of four claims. The Grahams and I developed deep, mutual respect. Since my house was only three or four miles from the Grahams' house, I would occasionally ride my bicycle to their house and stop in to see how they were doing. A few months after the repairs were completed, I stopped by to check in. All was well, they said, except their old dog finally passed. This was significant as the old dog was generating odors that by now engulfed each room in the house and was really strong in the sunroom. Today the house smelled a lot better.

A few weeks passed, and I got a phone call from Mr. Graham.

"I would like for you to stop by as soon as you can. We have another problem, and I need your help with it," he said.

"I have some free time right now. I'll be right over," I assured Mr. Graham.

I dropped what I was doing, made a phone call to rearrange my schedule, and drove immediately to the Grahams' residence.

"Hello, Leon, I am sorry to bother you, but I need some help," said Mr. Graham. "Come in and sit for a minute. I need to talk to you."

We went into the sunroom and sat.

Mrs. Graham started the conversation. "Leon, we have another claim filed for some water damage from our water heater. Mr. Graham has had a mild stroke and just got back from the hospital. He is doing fine now, but he is having some short-term memory issues. The other insurance company that we had our homeowner's policy with had to file bankruptcy, so we are now insured with a different insurance company. Can you work with this new company?"

"Ms. Graham, I have taken care of your house for, what, about two years now, and I have treated it like it was my own house and have done the very best to provide the very best materials and labor I can find. I promise that I will continue to treat your house with all the respect that you, Mr. Graham, and this beautiful home deserve."

I worked with the new insurance provider and was able to get a scope and price agreed on. This was a second-class carrier with third-rate adjusters who had marketed well but failed miserably to live up to their advertising, marketing, and hype.

Nevertheless, I worked through the situation, completed all the repairs, and got paid. During the repair time on this last project, Mr. Graham would call me and apologize, and then explain he had forgotten what we had discussed an hour before. I was patient, listened to my friend, and repeated discussions as many times as Mr. Graham asked me to.

Not long after the latest repair, I rode my bicycle by the Grahams to see how my friends were coming along.

"Hi, Leon," Mr. Graham greeted me. "Say, when are you going to buy this house?"

This had become somewhat of a joke between us as I had told Mr. Graham numerous times that I could not afford the property. I chuckled, "Okay, Mr. Graham, you have me at a weak point. I cannot afford this house but go ahead and tell me the price so we can end the discussion on this subject."

"Two hundred thousand. It's a bargain for that, and we would like for you to have our house. Now that means $200,000 in my pocket. You will have to pay all the closing costs and fees," he said.

The work I had performed on this beautiful Greek Mediterranean home had reached in excess of $50,000. I knew the house and had treated it like it was my own. The fifty-plus year-old house was in great shape. Mr. Graham and I shook hands with the understanding that I would buy their house but had to sell my other house first.

It took about a year for me to sell my house and buy the Grahams' phenomenal property. I moved in and immediately and began getting the landscape cleaned up, trimmed, and improved.

While business had been great, like many successful businesses, it attracted liars, thieves, and cowards. A few months after I bought the home, I discovered that my top executive had teamed up with my attorney and sent me into bankruptcy, then took over the construction business as I had been operating it, except with a change of name. I had not been happy in my new fantasy house; I didn't like my neighbors nor the traffic noise. It was quite a different experience living there day and night. I was on my usual morning walk when I saw real estate yard signs virtually everywhere. I called my real estate agent, Janie, to find out what was going on.

Janie did some research and called me, "This subdivision has become the hottest real estate around the Metroplex. It's selling for more than $125 a square foot, based on the heated and air-conditioned area."

I had just become aware of the severe damage my vice president of my company had done, and I desperately needed to sell the house, both for financial and emotional reasons. I learned that my vice president in charge of production was finishing each project with only one coat of paint as opposed to the two that it typically takes.. He had made it impossible to collect payments from the homeowners as each job appeared to be incomplete in some way.. He was doing substandard work in order to bankrupt me. I had borrowed the maximum at the bank to produce the work but couldn't collect. Suddenly, almost overnight, I realized I just did not belong in the city anymore.

I promptly filed for corporate bankruptcy. I sold the house for the full listing price in seven days and rented an apartment.

In the midst of all these crazy and rough times, I was about to experience the best thing that ever happened to me. I loved the outdoors. I frequented REI because they sold the toys I liked. They sold outdoor activity equipment from hiking socks to mountain climbing gear. REI had posted a flier about some new equipment. They offered classes to learn about these new products. I tried to sign up for the first class, but it was already full. I signed up for the second class offered. As the day arrived for the first class, I decided to go anyway just in case there had been a cancellation. As I walked into the demonstration room, I could see a lot of vacant seats. As I stepped through the doorway and to the right, I surveyed the room. As my gaze swept from left to right in the room, I locked eyes with a woman. It felt as though I had been hit with a laser beam. It was one of the most powerful first encounters I had ever known. I immediately made my way toward her. "Is this seat taken?" I asked. And those were the first words I said to my soulmate. I learned that Renee was coming out of a divorce. Her husband had been unfaithful and had been chasing every female who would let him. He had even begun staying all night at various places. Renee said she really did not want a divorce, but her patience was being pushed to the limit. Her husband came home one evening and informed her that his girlfriend was pregnant. Renee turned her body about 90 degrees and set up for a powerful Tae Kwon Do kick. She stepped toward him with her left foot and delivered a back kick to his ribs, effectively sending him flying over the couch and landing him on the floor on the other side.

I respected her ability to stand up for herself. I was getting into a better place emotionally and financially and was ready for a new adventure.

I had most everything paid for except for the house and car. I had owned the house for eighteen months and had made two or three modifications and dramatically enhanced the yard with landscaping and tree trimming. I was able to sell it for 150% percent over what I had paid for it. Now, I had a little extra money but wanted to keep most of it invested in real estate. I decided it was time to move back to the country where I was raised. I took a little money out of the proceeds from the sale of the house and paid a couple of small debts.

I was now debt free, except for my Suburban. I spent weekend after weekend driving the roads of Central Texas, west of Waco, where I found a small rundown ranch and bought it. Finally, I had made it, albeit **the long way around**, back to the country. I bought it but was not able to move there fulltime right away.

Renee and I stuck together like Velcro. Early on, it was a match — little did we know just how much we were alike. It was as if we were one spirit, in mind and in thought. Renee had graduated from University of Texas at Dallas, and I had graduated from University of Texas at Arlington. Her graduating GPA (3.7), however, was a few points above my (3.0). I had tested for third-degree red belt, passed, and had been given an honorary black belt from my teacher, who said he should have given it to me long before. He told me I was the best student he'd ever had in his twenty-four years of teaching. Renee, also a Tae Kwon Do student, attended a school that used brown belts to be the same level as red. Renee had been training for and was ready for her black belt test. I had been a part of the American Organization of Karate (AOK). Renee had trained and competed in the Traditional Karate League (TKL). She was somewhat distracted because of her separation and divorce. She had also acquired me as a new companion. She needed focus. I had the answers and knew how to help her. The belt test was a few days away, so we got busy preparing.

The day of the belt test, six adult males showed up to test with Renee for first-degree black belt. Without a doubt, Renee quickly established that she was the best of the seven. She was faster, had better balance, better flexibility, better form, and was just better prepared mentally and physically for the test. Like me, she was an overachiever. I had introduced meditation to Renee and led her through a few meditations to help her reduce her anxieties and stay focused on a very, very important test. It has been said that only one of every one hundred thousand who start taking lessons in the martial arts make it to the level of black belt. A true black belt is an exceptional individual in more ways than just blocking, punching, and kicking. A **true** black belt demonstrates a level of character and integrity that is above and beyond that of the average citizen.

Renee really demonstrated her physical and mental abilities in the four grueling hours of testing. She was nothing short of amazing. Who's this woman, Superwoman? The connection between Renee and me only got better; in fact, after twenty-five years of being together, our love and respect for each other continues to grow. These were easily the best years of my life, and Renee said the same thing about her life.

She really proved her mettle the first time we went grocery shopping together. I was driving my new black Suburban and pulled into the Kroger parking lot. As I was maneuvering to find a parking spot, two young males were walking slowly, blocking the driveway and traffic. I bumped the car horn to get them to move out of the way. As they moved to the right, I drove slowly past them, and they gave me a "go to hell" look. I parked about a hundred feet down the aisle. As Renee and I got out of my Suburban, these two young men began running toward us. She blocked the first attacker and let the other advance toward me. I quickly got around to her side and waited until this idiot got close enough, then I placed my index and middle fingers of my left hand just under his eyes, firmly hitting his cheekbones, totally shocking him. He stopped dead in his tracks. He desperately needed a lesson In manners, maybe he learned from this. I might have been a large-framed man, forty-seven years old and wearing a thirty-six-inch sleeve length, but my hands were as quick as a rattlesnake strike. I achieved my goal, which was to scare the hell out of this dumbass kid without hurting him. I could have easily permanently disabled this young man but thought better of it.

As time went on, Renee and I grew even closer. Sometimes we were both in the same city, and there were times that we traveled separately, sometimes a couple of thousand miles or more apart. Sometimes we would be in the house or car together, but no matter whether we were close or thousands of miles apart, we were always thinking the same thing. I would be thinking about Italian food, and Renee would say, "I was thinking about Italian food, too." Virtually every time one of us mentioned our thoughts, the other would say, "I was thinking the same thing." After more than twenty-five years together, nothing has changed. It's as if our brains are hard wired together.

Though we lived separately at first, she was either at my place, or I was at hers. We decided that I would move in with her. I needed to get productive and start earning an income, as I wanted to conserve some cash. After I moved into Renee's house, I decided to take some real estate classes. I asked her if she was interested in taking a real estate class or two with me. I was pleasantly surprised that she was. While she had graduated from the university with a higher grade point average than I had, each time we took a test, I seemed to be able to score just a little higher.

I was also an expert shot with firearms and continued to have a lot of pent-up anger toward the three who had bankrupted me. I felt I would have been justified in killing a couple of those involved, but as the old saying goes: "Don't do the crime if you don't want to do the time." No way in hell was I going to ruin the rest of my life over three liars, thieves, and cowards. The emotional toll was heavy. Renee wanted to wait awhile to get married because she could sense and feel my frustration and anger. Also, she did not want to have to visit her husband in prison. We waited patiently.

Renee and I took classes, and I got my real estate sales license. With my license in hand, I immediately began making money selling houses in Grapevine, Southlake, and the Keller area near Fort Worth. The real estate market was really hot in those areas of the Metroplex. Since I had been working so closely with members of the property and casualty businesses, I had also taken a class a couple of years earlier and had passed the state test to be a licensed property casualty adjuster. With this license, I was ready to chase storm claims. I signed up with as many independent adjustment firms as I could, to get some experience as a storm adjuster. I had been doing that job when I was a contractor, but now I would read the policies and explain coverage to the policyholders.

On my family front, my younger son had graduated from Texas A & M University with a degree in veterinary medicine. After a couple of years in the field working for a couple of different veterinarians, he decided to take a position at a major university and became a professor in veterinary medicine. Both of my boys were now doctors. I could not have been prouder.

Renee and I continued to grow together as we developed a mutual admiration society of our own. We got married, which was redundant, as we were joined at the hip. I was going to do whatever it took to keep this girl around, and she had developed the same love and admiration for me.

We continued to live in Grapevine as I sold residential real estate and made trips to the ranch on weekends and holidays. I didn't care a lot for residential real estate sales, so I began shifting my focus to farm and ranch. Not long after making this shift in focus, I was called to work a storm in North Carolina. A friend covered my listings while I was gone. I worked storms here and there but had not connected with a company that had the volume of work that I wanted. In 2003 Hurricane Isabel hit Virginia, and I was called to work this storm. It was a busy time with lots of changes in the air: Renee had been offered an early retirement at Verizon. The real estate market was hot. I had told Renee that I loved her dearly but that I was tired of living in the city and wanted to take up residence at the ranch full time. I had established a relationship with a real estate broker in Waco who would let me do my thing while he covered my listings when I needed to travel. So, with all my talents and energy, I worked storm claims as often as I could and worked real estate in between. I also spent as much time as I could working on the broken-down old ranch. Renee would help, and together we would disassemble old, falling-down buildings and clean up old fencing and brush. We were able to move full time to the ranch, as Renee had accepted the buyout from Verizon. We sold the house in Grapevine for full list price in a week and headed for the ranch.

After more than twenty-five years in the city, I was finally returning to the country — where I started my journey and where I would find another level of peace in my heart. Renee and I loved being at the ranch and welcomed our new perspectives and goals. Retired from Verizon, she got her adjuster's license, and for the next six years we traveled together working claims for State Farm and USAA. We worked hurricane claims along the gulf coast to southern Florida and up the east coast to Maryland. We worked hail and tornado claims from San Antonio to Michiana, Indiana. With the help of my broker, I also sold a few farm and ranch listings in and around Hamilton, Comanche, Lampasas, and Coryell counties.

Around 2009, Renee suggested that I stay at the ranch and work there while she traveled. She finally landed a gig at the State

Farm regional office in Dallas. That allowed her to come home every Saturday night and get up at 3:30 Monday morning so she could be back at the office at 7 a.m. I sometimes would make the three-hour drive to Dallas on weekends.

The ranch kept me busy and working hard. I cleaned up over two hundred acres of prickly pear cactus and cedar. I sprayed the smaller mesquite and even did some weed spraying. The Farm Service Agency's soil and conservation department helped with this. Due to erosion and e coli issues, I was funded on two projects, which totaled about $120,000. When we were nearly finished building five miles of fence, planting two hundred and twenty-five acres of improved grasses, and installing two miles of water line, a tornado hit our place, causing about $50,000 in property and contents damage.

I had put the ranch up for sale a few years earlier, as I was getting older, and Renee and I were thinking about retiring. I had turned the run down-old ranch into what might have been the most productive ranch around. I sold out my cattle for about $150,000. I also sold some of the other equipment such as my Lincoln pipeline welder, my forty-five-foot boom sprayer, and things of that sort.

Covid hit in 2020, and everybody wanted to get out of the city.

We sold the ranch for a handsome profit. When I was leasing the ranch in the early years, I had built a herd of Brangus. The cows, calves, and especially the bulls took me back to my childhood and made me remember the milk cows I helped raise.

With the ranch sold, we needed a new place to settle. We had spent many a weekend in and around Fredericksburg, Texas, and loved it, so we downsized from four hundred acres to four acres just outside Fredericksburg. We did get a little bigger house.

We now ride our Harley in the Hill Country and travel some here and there. We're getting older but are able to get most of our age-related problems taken care of.

When I consider my childhood of poverty and abuse and then look at where I am today, I am overcome with emotion. I am grateful for all the experiences that helped shape me, for all the opportunities that came my way, and for the fortitude in my heart and soul that kept me going and kept returning me to the path I was meant to follow. I am proud to have lived an honest life, for having stayed true to myself. Today, Renee and I are content; we want for nothing, and I have no regrets.

The house on Park Avenue that
I eventually sold. I used the money from the
sale to put a down payment on the farm.

My and Renee's wedding day,
the happiest day of my life.

My racing days.

My first dirt track car.

The car I built when I was 41.

Epilogue

My story takes a hard stance on the Mormon church, and it does so with good reason, based on my experience. I've heard that it is harder to escape Mormonism than it is to get out of the Mafia. I agree. I see Mormonism as a cult.

Like other religions and cults, the Mormons practice rituals and ceremonies, and through these practices, children, teenagers, and adults are fed subtle messages, similar to the way a hypnotist makes suggestions. In the case of Mormonism, I call these practices brainwashing. In the Mormon religion, a child is subjected to these activities just after he or she is born, and the practices continue throughout a person's life. The power of suggestion is a powerful thing, especially if the individual is feeling vulnerable.

At the age of twenty-four, I had had enough praying, enough rituals, and enough ceremonies. I had never subscribed to the Mormon philosophy of turning the other cheek when I was assaulted. I felt as if I might burst, so I left the Mormon cult. When I left, of course, they turned against me. My ex-family and the Mormons taught my two boys that I was possessed by the devil. My own family really gave me hell, and years later they still tell outrageous lies about me.

I needed an emotional outlet, and I found that through meditation. After I learned about meditation and developed my skills, I gained an ability to listen. Where I had lived a life of guilt and turmoil, I found a way to find peace. Peace in your heart and clarity of the mind are not easy things for most people to find. And for those who do find it, the peace and clarity can be fleeting. I learned that my meditations helped me in every way to manage living in a world of chaos. Meditation helps me prepare for a night's sleep. I always go to sleep quicker and sleep more peacefully when I meditate before I go to sleep. I meditated before many exams at the university. I meditated a lot in preparing for a Tae Kwon Do tournament. I even meditated briefly before many matches.

Prayer was different. I learned to pray early on, the Mormon way. Praying was always talking. Praying was always asking. Praying was thanking. Meditation is listening. With all the praying I grew up around, there was never a suggestion that someone should listen. We were given two ears, two eyes, and one mouth. This suggests to me that we should listen and observe at least four times as much as we talk.

I began writing this memoir at our ranch when I was about sixty-eight years old. My wife was working out of town, so I had a lot of alone time. By this time, I had accumulated a couple of meditation cushions, which allowed me to kneel and sit while meditating. I also read a book on how to find happiness, written by the Dalai Lama. The more I meditated, the more answers I found to questions that had plagued me. Many of the times and events in my life were traumatic, so it was hard to reach back in time and recall those emotionally charged events. This manuscript has been one of the most cathartic exercises I have experienced. Life gives us all bruises, cuts, and scars. Some feel the bruises and cuts more deeply, and some carry and feel the deep scars their entire lives. As they say, it is not where you start; it is where you finish.

I am embarrassed and, in some cases, ashamed of my failures. I made a lot of bad decisions in my early life. Meditation allows me to forgive myself and move on. There is a fine line between remembering and forgiving. When remembering abuse, it makes it hard to find forgiveness. Most people are born, live a life of ignorance, and die without changing a bit, blindly following what they were taught. I am thankful that I found enlightenment, which has helped me elevate myself from poverty to a level that, while not rich, is amply comfortable and lacking in nothing. I have achieved what others find unachievable. I did this by putting one foot in front of the other, regardless of how hard that was to do at times. When I'd recognize that my direction was off, I would stop and hit the *reset* button and get back on track. When I made a commitment, there was no turning back. When I made the decision to quit a promising career as a carpenter and go back to school, I was completely committed. In my mind, I'd blown up the roads and burned the bridges, so there was nowhere to turn back to! I was as committed as one can get.

As soon as I turned my focus to the future, lots of good things happened. Until then, I'd kept looking back to find answers, and this confused me because of the mixed messages my early teaching gave me. I also stumbled and fell a lot because looking back does not allow you to look ahead and see the obstacles. As it has been said, the past is gone and is now history. The future is uncertain. Today is a gift and that is why it is called the *present*.

Meditation brings the meditator to the present. Meditation early as the sun rises in the morning is the prime time to assess your position in life or to alter it. This was and is an ideal meditation time for me. I used to be out on the ranch at sunrise with the cows during calving season. It was a time of quiet serenity, a perfect environment for meditation. Meditation is a way to really get to know yourself, and as Bruce Lee said, that is the most important thing in life. Being calm and peaceful allows for the brain to function at its maximum ability. When I start the day with meditation, things just seem to fall into place a little better.

I hope that my story shows readers how one can find peace, no matter how rocky the road that leads to it. I hope that anyone struggling to overcome an abusive childhood will find in my story the courage to seek their own destinies.